Wessex Dialect

NORMAN ROGERS **Wessex Dialect**

MOONRAKER PRESS

© 1979 Norman Rogers

First published in 1979 by Moonraker Press
26 St Margarets Street, Bradford-on-Avon, Wiltshire

SBN 239.00182.6

Text set in 11/12 pt Photon Times, printed by photolithography,
and bound in Great Britain at The Pitman Press, Bath

CONTENTS

1   Introduction   *page*   1

2   The Phonetic Alphabet   12

3   Pronunciation   15

4   Grammar   31

5   Vocabulary   43

6   Dialect and Society   52

    Glossary of Dialect Words   71

    Appendix: list of linguistic terms   93

    Bibliography   97

PREFACE

The origin of this book was a series of notes I made in the late 1950s and early 1960s on my own dialect. Although I had had some training in phonetics and historical grammar, it soon became apparent that new ideas and techniques for describing languages which had been developed after the first World War, too late to be included in the courses I had followed, would be most useful to me in my project. I therefore embarked on a course of reading to bring myself up-to-date. In reading, I found much that concerned my profession as a language teacher and felt impelled to follow that line of study. Increasing responsibilities, both to my job and to my family, prevented me from making further progress in dialect studies. In the meantime, the basic material of the Leeds University Survey of English Dialects was published, a landmark in the study of English vernaculars.

I was, therefore, very pleased when I was asked to produce a book for publication by Moonraker Press, as it enabled me to resume an interest of many years' standing. The dialect of west Wiltshire was my first language, learnt in a dialect-speaking family in a largely dialect-speaking community. Contact with older people, especially my grand-parents, gave me a good idea of the dialect spoken not long after the middle of the nineteenth century, when many features that have disappeared today were still intact. It was obvious, of course, that knowledge of the dialect of a particular area does not entitle one to write about south-western dialects in general, any more than a knowlege of English is enough to write about European languages, so I had to consult such material as was available, mainly the Leeds Dialect Survey and the publications of the now-defunct English Dialect Society. A brief account of the history of dialect studies is given in chapter 1, and a full list of books in the bibliography.

I was encouraged to find that my original notes formed a sound base for this book, but I must express my gratitude to the Institute of Dialect and Folk Life Studies, University of Leeds, the Director, Mr S. F. Sanderson, M.A. and Messrs E. J. Arnold & Son, the publishers, for permission to use material taken from their *Survey of English Dialects, the Basic Material*, volume 2 for Gloucestershire, and volume 4 for the other counties.

Many of us drive cars but have little or no knowledge of what goes on under the bonnet. Equally, although we are all past-masters at speaking our native tongue, we do not all possess the necessary analytical information to understand fully the whys and wherefores of language. Language is a very technical subject which has been studied intensively during the course of the past hundred years, and new techniques of analysis and a new vocabulary of terms have been developed. To avoid the new findings and to ignore the new terms is to run the risk of being vague and imprecise; to lard one's text with the latest jargon is to put the book beyond the reach of the average educated reader. I have tried to steer a middle course, using the terms where necessary, but explaining them in the text and in a short list at the end of the book. I have also thought it wise to use symbols of the International Phonetic Alphabet, for reasons given in chapter 2.

We now have a well developed science of language, but it deals not with the unchanging and universal phenomena of physics or mathematics, but with the variable and elusive facts of a behavioural science. Our varied lives and experiences impart many indiosyncratic twists to the way we speak, in both pronunciation and meaning, and this had led linguists to say that the only true analysis is that of one utterance made at one time by one person. This gives a very narrow viewpoint and, especially for the general reader, a broader approach is more valuable. I have tried to give a picture of dialect as used over the past century, that is during the lifetime of older people living now and that of their parents who taught them to speak.

In 1896, the English Dialect Society, having compiled a dictionary and grammar, in addition to a number of works on small areas, felt that its task was complete, and it disbanded. Eighty years later, even following the publication of the basic material of the Leeds Survey, we cannot share their satisfaction. Much more research needs to be done on, to take but one example, the distribution of local words and the way their meaning varies from region to region. Much interest is shown in northern counties in local speech, and Lancashire and Yorkshire have active Dialect Societies. I hope that the publication of this book may awaken a little of that interest in the south-west.

Finally, I should like to thank my brother, Mr K. H. Rogers, for reading through the typescript and for making many valuable suggestions, and my wife for checking the text for mistakes and putting them right.

Note: The place names in this book refer to the historical English counties, not to the newly set-up administrative districts. N.R.

This book is about the dialect spoken in the south-western counties of England. Dialect, to most people, means a regional variant of standard speech, but today linguists talk also of 'class dialects' and 'trade dialects'. The term, like so many others in the study of languages, is hard to define rigorously. Later in this chapter I shall attempt to describe the characteristics of English regional dialects in general, and south-western dialects in particular but, first, it would be useful to take a brief look at the English language, its history and how it is used at the present day.

English is a Germanic language. That is, it resembles in many important respects such languages as German, Dutch, Swedish, Icelandic and others. This is because these languages are descended from one parent language, called Common Germanic, which was spoken in Northern Europe about 2,400 years ago. Gradually differences began to appear in the speech of various communities, due to their isolation one from the other. Because of these changes we can now say that several dialects had arisen. These differences increased to the point where one community found the speech of another community unintelligible, so that the dialects had become different languages.

Common Germanic itself had descended in the same way from a parent language—now lost—which linguistic historians call 'Proto-Indo-European', and from which the majority of European languages, as well as others from the Middle East and India, are derived. They are known as Indo-European languages.

English was brought to this country by the Anglo-Saxons in the fifth, sixth and seventh centuries A.D. When they arrived, they found a native population speaking Celtic languages, another branch of the Indo-European group and from which Welsh, Scots Gaelic and Irish have come. To this branch, too, belongs the ancient Cornish language, which died out in the eighteenth century as a living tongue, but of which written forms still exist. Since the arrival of the Anglo-Saxons our language has changed out of all recognition, and for a modern Englishman learning Anglo-Saxon, or Old English as it is now considered more correct to call it, is equivalent to learning a foreign language.

The reasons why languages change are not clearly understood. We can, however, pinpoint certain factors in the development of English. One very important influence was the influx into the North and East of Britain of large numbers of Norsemen—the Vikings. Their language bore many resemblances to Anglo-Saxon, and contact between the two peoples brought about a considerable simplification of Anglo-Saxon grammar. Our ancestors used word-endings, or 'inflexions', to indicate the function of a word in a sentence, rather like Latin or present-day German or Russian. Vikings and Anglo-Saxons found that they could understand each other if not too much stress was placed on the word ending, and thus began a process of decay which has caused the virtual disappearance of inflexions from our language; we still use -'s to show possession, -ed to show past tense and the -s in the present tense (e.g. 'he goes') but these are remnants of a once complicated system.

For 300 years after the defeat of Harold at Hastings in 1066, French was the language of the Court and the nobility but not of the common people. French had little influence on the basic structure of our language, but large numbers of words were borrowed into English. This meant that we had two words for the same thing, but the pairs usually took on a different meaning, sometimes very different, such as *sheep* (Anglo-Saxon sceap) and *mutton* (French mouton), sometimes with a more subtle distinction as *folk* (Anglo-Saxon folc) and *people* (French peuple).

Borrowings took place, too, from other languages—Latin, the language of medieval scholarship, and the many languages our empire-builders and traders came into contact with. Pronunciation also has changed considerably, sometimes slowly, sometimes rapidly. One period of rapid change was in the early years of the sixteenth century, when there were widespread modifications in vowel sounds. These last changes are known as the 'Great Vowel Shift'.

Throughout the Anglo-Saxon and Middle English period (i.e. up to the end of the fifteenth century), regional dialects were spoken by everyone of whatever degree. Sir Walter Raleigh, we are told, spoke in his Devonshire dialect at court until his death, although the fact that this was worth noting shows that the position was changing in the reign of Elizabeth I. We know the dialects of these periods only through the varying spelling of texts written in different areas. During the Anglo-Saxon period, most of the extant texts were written in the West Saxon dialect, reminding us that Wessex was the last stronghold of the English when the Danes held much of the rest of England.

The Anglo-Saxon dialects developed into the Middle English dialects, with considerable regional variations. It was not always easy, or even possible, to understand someone from a different part of England. Caxton, in his Prologue to his *Eynedos* tells of merchants from

Northamptonshire who were becalmed off the Kent coast. They rowed ashore and asked for 'eggys'. The good wife whom they had addressed told them to be about their business as she did not speak French: in Kent the plural of egg was 'eyren'.

The modern period needs close scrutiny. In the sixteenth century the dialect of the East Midlands began to assume a special prestige. The area contained the University towns of Oxford and Cambridge, and London and the King's court lay on the edge. This dialect became the language of scholars and of courtiers, and has developed into 'standard English' or 'B.B.C. English'. It is known as 'Received Standard' (R.S. for short), and the pronunciation is called 'Received Pronunciation' (R.P.). This is the language of books, printed documents, newspapers and of 'educated' speakers.

That there should be a supra-regional dialect, used in writing and in formal communication, was a new idea in English. It became, as well, a class symbol, adopted by the upper classes, and perpetuated in Public School education. Families who rose in prosperity looked for a more acceptable mode of expression, and a rise in status often meant the adoption by the children of R.P. Dialect-speaking parents usually encouraged this change. Fifty years ago most educated people used R.P. but, today, regional accents have become much more acceptable and varying degrees of accent are heard in the speech of University teachers, politicians and B.B.C. interviewers, for example.

It has long been assumed that broad dialect speakers are rapidly getting fewer in number. Investigations, both in this century and the last have had an air of urgency about them and informants have been chosen from elderly people of rural background. Little has been done to find out about the speech of younger people or of those who live in cities. The present situation is only a matter for conjecture. It seems that many dialectal characteristics are indeed disappearing under the influence of the 'media', universal education and ease of movement between different parts of the country. But a certain amount survives, not so much in the realms of grammar or vocabulary as in the phonology, the pronunciation that gives us our regional accents.

Another fact we must note about our language at the present time is that R.S. is standard English, and little variation is possible if one is to speak correctly. Some choice is left to the speaker—the exact position of adverbs in a sentence is an example—but on the whole he has to conform to the rules. This degree of standardisation does not exist in dialect. Just as we note with amazement that in old manuscripts the same word may be spelt in two different ways in the same sentence, we may hear the same word pronounced in two different ways by the same dialect speaker. Edward Slow, the Salisbury poet, pointed out that the word 'home' could be pronounced as 'wom, wimm or whoam' even in the same village, and in the dialogue he appends to his note to illustrate the fact, Bob says 'wom' and 'whoam', while Zam, in his reply says 'wimm'.

The English language today is not just a choice between dialect and R.S. and R.P. These might be seen as two poles between which lies a whole spectrum of forms of speech that we may call colloquial English. Examples range from the use of the word 'got' which some purists will not accept as 'good' English (I was not allowed to use the word at school), to sentences such as 'I ain't told no lies', which are heard over most of England.

Another point to be noted is the use of 'registers'. This means the ability we all possess of suiting our speech to the person we are addressing. 'Come off it' and 'I fancy your Grace may have been misled' mean much the same thing, but only the second is suitable for an Archbishop. The dialect speaker was always an adept at changing registers. J. Kjederqvist, in his account of the dialect of Pewsey in Wiltshire (published in 1902) says: 'One difficulty of obtaining real dialect pronunciation is included in the fact that the peasantry throughout the country usually have two different pronunciations, one which they use to one another, and one which they use to the educated.' Dialect, too, has a vocabulary for talking to children, parallel with the 'bunny-rabbits' or the 'gee-gees' of standard English.

Another unusual feature of present-day English is the fact of almost universal literacy. Printed texts provide examples of literary English, which set a standard of correctness. One effect has been that change in the language has been slowed up. However, literacy has brought certain changes in pronunciation—these are spelling pronunciations, words being pronounced as they are spelled. An example of this is the word *waistcoat*, now pronounced as if the two words *waist* and *coat* were joined together. The older pronunciation is [wɛskɪt]. (See chapter 2 for an explanation of the International Phonetic Alphabet which has been used here.) Place names have been very much affected by this tendency to spelling pronunciations. Cirencester in Gloucestershire has lost its old pronunciation of 'Zisister' and Hardenhuish in Wiltshire is now pronounced as it is spelled, rather than 'Harnish' as formerly.

We must not, however, let the written form of the language mislead us about pronunciation. We write *bread and butter* as three distinct words, but we almost always say 'brem butter' ([brɛmbʌtə] in phonetic notation.) This is because the movements made by the tongue and the lips in speech are very quick, and tend to run into each other, by-passing certain sounds and amalgamating others. In the example given, the raising of the tongue to touch the top of the mouth just behind the teeth, necessary to make the [d] sound, is omitted, and the vowels of *bread* and *and* are joined. The [n] sound, which should have been heard in *and* is a nasal consonant because part of the sound is directed through the nose, the [b] sound in *butter* is a labial consonant, i.e. it is made with the lips. In our phrase, we are in too great a hurry, and we close the lips as sound is passing through the nose, thus producing [m], a labio-nasal consonant. This process, the running together of the movements necessary to make sounds, is called 'assimilation' and we shall meet it in dialect—in, for instance, *oven*, pronounced sometimes [ʌvm], where the labial (lip) element of [v] changes [n] to [m].

Today, we are used to the idea of national languages. When we learn French, we expect to be understood from Calais in the North to Nice in the South, and as soon as we cross the Italian frontier we expect to hear Italian spoken. Formerly, linguistic boundaries were not so well marked as they are today and languages blended into one another. This is the position with dialects. As we move further from our own region, we notice that speech characteristics disappear and are replaced, one by one, until we are aware of a completely different dialect. Dialect studies are often 'Linguistic Geography' and the aim is to produce an atlas showing in which areas features of pronunciation, grammar and vocabulary are to be found. These areas are delineated by 'isoglosses'. Isoglosses are lines similar to geographical isobars or isotherms, joining the farthest points at which a dialect feature is noticed. In southern England it would be necessary to plot isoglosses to show where initial f is pronounced like v, or initial s like z, two important characteristics of the area we are dealing with. Isoglosses interweave in a bewildering and complex fashion, and the two mentioned above, although the sound changes are similar (voicing of an unvoiced consonant) by no means coincide. In certain places a number of isoglosses run together, and this 'bundling' marks off one dialect area from another. Needless to say, bundles of isoglosses hardly ever coincide with county boundaries in spite of the fact that it has long been common practice to speak of 'the Somersetshire dialect' or 'a Dorset accent'.

Interest in linguistic theory was almost non-existent in western Europe until the middle of the eighteenth century. Then the realisation that resemblances between languages could not be accidental sparked off a massive effort by many first-class scholars. In the eighteenth and nineteenth centuries they concentrated on the historical development of languages. That study has continued into this century, but the emphasis has shifted to how best to describe a language or how to teach it.

Information about dialects in the seventeenth and eighteenth centuries is not easy to find. Some can be obtained from the writings of men who taught elegant speech, and we find lists of pronunciations that they condemn as being too provincial. There was, too, an increasing number of glossaries of local words published, but it was in the nineteenth century that the first systematic study of English dialects was made. The impetus came from work already in progress on the Continent and also from the feeling that dialect was disappearing and ought be recorded before it was too late. Joseph Wright, Professor of Comparative Philology at Oxford University, and one of the great dialectologists, wrote in 1895: 'Pure dialect is disappearing even in the country districts, owing to the spread of education and to the modern facilities of inter-communication.' However, he could still write in 1926: 'It is very difficult to find people who can speak dialect without being seriously mixed with the standard language.' While there is no doubt that what Wright wrote is true, dialects seem to have been more tenacious than was imagined at the time.

Another famous name of the nineteenth century is the Reverend Walter Skeat, who founded in 1873 the English Dialect Society. The Society published works, mainly glossaries, on individual counties. The names of those relevant to our region will be found listed in the bibliography at the end of this book, but as an example I should like to mention here the studies of the dialect of West Somersetshire by J. Elworthy, as being one of the most informative and easy to read. A. J. Ellis devoted the fifth volume of his work *On Early English Pronunciation* to a complete survey of dialect phonology, but the main product of these studies was the publication by the English Dialect Society in 1898 of the English Dialect Dictionary in six volumes, incorporating an English Dialect Grammar, later published separately. Having done this, the Society felt that its task was completed, and it disbanded. Further local surveys in the same tradition were written after this date, among which we may mention one of the dialect of Pewsey in Wiltshire, by J. Kjederqvist (1902), *Studies in the Dorset Dialect*, by B. Widen (1949) and a *Grammar of the Dialect of West Somerset*, by E. Kruisinga (1905).

The work of these men is painstaking and thorough, but the findings of the earlier ones have to be handled with care. They have no doubt recorded many facts which would otherwise have been lost, but they lacked an adequate theoretical basis for the study of language, and their techniques for gathering information were primitive. For instance, they had no standard form of phonetic notation to describe pronunciation, and the individual alphabets they used are often difficult to interpret. They obtained information by means of a postal questionnaire sent, not to dialect speakers, but to educated people in the locality, the majority of whom were recording speech sounds for the first time in their lives. It is not to be wondered at that there were many mistakes. And they located their findings according to counties, an approach not nearly precise enough in modern eyes. Lastly they were concerned with the historical aspect of dialect and listed, for example, the sound changes in any district according to the vowel the word had in Anglo-Saxon or Middle English. This makes it difficult for the general reader to understand these rather scholarly works.

The study of dialect has continued and gained strength in the present century. Various articles and monographs have been published, but they have all been dwarfed by the Survey of English Dialects carried out by Leeds University. The survey was based on a questionnaire drawn up by Professor Harold Orton of Leeds and Professor Eugen Dieth of Zurich. Locations were chosen, covering the whole of England. The number in our area varies from five in Dorsetshire to 13 in Somersetshire. Trained field-workers visited each chosen location and found a resident, one who had spent his whole life in the area, who was willing to act as informant. The field-worker recorded in phonetic script the answers given. Tape recorders were also used to preserve the speech of selected informants. So far, five volumes have been published, an introduction and four volumes of basic material. The basic material consists of all the responses listed according to counties, with a minimum of comment. The south-western counties are contained in the fourth volume, Southern England, with the exception of Gloucestershire, which is in the West-Midland volume (the classification of counties into the four volumes has no significance). The publication of a Linguistic Atlas is planned, showing, by means of isoglosses, the area in which dialect features are noted. An Atlas has been published in Switzerland covering the northern region. (My impression is that northern dialects have, in general, received more attention than those in our area.)

This survey has added much to our knowledge of dialect, but work still remains to be done. The Leeds questionnaire was drawn up for the whole of England and the compilers went to great lengths not to suggest words to informants, asking, for example, about 'animals that give milk' rather than 'cows', for fear that the investigator might influence the informant's pronunciation or choice of words. Some questions did not get the answer they might have. For instance, the word *keck*, to retch, was commonly used in Wiltshire when I was a child but was only recorded once in Berkshire, and not at all in Wiltshire, and *kecker*, the throat, was not noted at all. There is a danger, too, that the idiosyncracies of an individual speaker may be enshrined as dialect. It is difficult to graft dialect words on to sentences conceived in R.S. One question was put in the form of a sentence 'If you have apples, you . . . them'. This did not get the reply I would have expected, *d'eat*. The same sentence in dialect runs 'If you got apples you d'eat 'em'. It seems to me that, ideally, a second survey should be made, concentrating on the features known to exist in the area, and using a larger number of informants, asking not 'What do you say when you are going to be sick?', but 'Do you know or use the word *keck*?'

The relationship between investigator and informant is not always an easy one, and a great deal of skill is needed to put the latter at his ease, so that he does not 'talk grand', or as Elworthy put it, 'to effectually shut himself up in an impenetrable shell of company manners and awkward mimicry of what he supposes to be jin.l.voaks wai oa spaikin'. The last few words are of course, 'gentlefolk's way of speaking' and illustrate the kind of phonetic notation used in the last century. One cannot always escape the impression that nineteenth-century investigators were a little patronising towards their informants. J. Kjederqvist says in his rather pompous way of his informant, Joseph Cripps, '. . . so all I had to do was to use him with the precaution necessary not to make him my real teacher, although my superior in the matter taught, that is, to lead him so that he was not always quite aware of the point on which he was really giving information'. The rather more jovial Elworthy comments on the phrase *Baewd u feeftee puyp* (about a fifty pipe): 'This last expression would convey a definite idea to a native—no vision of Broseley or Meerschaum would confuse his brain, nor would a thought of luscious port occur to him, but only common draining pipes'. An interesting account of the relationship between informant and investigator, though not in the sphere of dialect research, but of rural life in general, is given in W. H. Hudson's *A Shepherd's Life*.

In the Anglo-Saxon and Middle English periods all writing was necessarily in dialect, as no standard language existed, but as we have seen the East-Midland dialect has developed into R.S. used in writing at the present day. For the last three or four hundred years, regional dialects have rarely influenced the written language, and communities that must have been dialect-speaking produced documents—deeds, account books, wills etc.—in the standard English of the day. There are exceptions, but they are few and far between—local words used in vestry minutes or the odd dialectal verb form. However, there has been some dialect literature, that is when an author uses dialect as a stylistic device. In a bibliography of Somerset works in the British Museum Library are listed polemical works written in the dialect of that county in the seventeenth century, including *A phantaisie or conceit between Tom-asse Pragmaticus and Nick-all-asse Non-sense* (1641) and *The Western Husbandman's Lament* (1645). The nineteenth century saw a large number of writers who experimented in dialect verse, but the majority of them are now only read as curiosities. Thomas Hardy is a novelist and poet of real stature associated with West-country dialect in his tales of Dorsetshire, and Eden Philpotts writes of Devonshire. Another, less known, but deserving mention is the Rev. William Barnes who wrote poems in the Dorset dialect, including the famous Linden Lea, set to music by Vaughan-Williams. The difficulty of writing in dialect is that no standardised spelling exists, and authors have to use makeshift orthography. This is usually adequate enough to recall to the dialect speaker the pronunciation the author intended, but it often leaves the non-dialect speaker puzzled over the exact value of a vowel or a consonant. Tennyson wrote poems in the dialect of Lincolnshire, and it is a salutary experience for a West-country man to try to read them aloud.

When we speak of language, we refer to millions of daily utterances by millions of people, using a medium that has developed over hundreds of years. Inevitably, there is much variation and the scientific precision associated with Physics or Mathematics is lacking. So statements that are generally true are difficult to make and one has usually to qualify what one says with 'often', 'for the most part' or 'mainly'. Categories, too, overlap and are not well defined. For instance, in the sentence 'Sawing this wood is hard work', is sawing a noun, because it is the subject of the sentence, or is it a verb, because it has a direct object? Arbitrary choices have to be made in many cases. Taking into account that no man is really consistent in his speech, linguists say that the only true description is that of one utterance of one man at one time. Be that as it may, it makes any meaningful account of a language or a dialect impossible. In any case, a man's experience of language extends well beyond himself (in the speech of the people he meets during the course of his life), and well beyond his own lifetime (in the speech of the people older than he). I have vivid recollections of the dialect of men and women who were in their eighties when I was a child, especially of my grand-parents, and so who learned to speak in the mid-nineteenth century. In this book I have decided to describe the forms of speech used and heard between the year 1900 and the present day, although I shall refer to earlier features when they are of interest.

In the reference quoted above J. Kjederqvist distinguished between the speech the 'peasantry' used to each other and the one they used to the 'educated'. Most writers on dialect have been educated and therefore had to rely on informants, noting and analysing their speech. In fact, some made a virtue out of necessity, and insisted that this was the only acceptable method, ruling out 'introspection' (i.e. using your own experience) as being much too unreliable. As a native dialect speaker, I intend to draw widely on my own knowledge of West Country speech. I have, of course consulted such books as are available, including the Leeds Survey of English Dialects, and these are listed in the bibliography at the end of this book.

We may now take a general look at modern English dialects. They exist in speech, hardly ever in writing. Such written works as have been produced are not really satisfactory because of the spelling difficulty.

English dialects have not become mutually unintelligible, as did those of Common Germanic. This is because there has always been much contact between the inhabitants of the various parts of Great Britain, and much borrowing between dialects. The word 'they' used very commonly in the West country, and in so characteristic a fashion (as a demonstrative, e.g. *Look at they cows*) came into our language from Scandinavia, first into the Northern dialects from which it spread south in the Middle English period. In the last few hundred years R.S. has provided a unifying factor. Dialect speakers, of course, know and understand R.S., and use it in writing.

Dialect is very much more varied than standard English. This may be random variation, i.e. the speaker chooses one form or another according to his whim at the time, or it may be regional variation. It must be appreciated that we are not dealing with a neat, well defined situation but an exceedingly complex one. Some of the characteristics to be described cover only a part of our area, some omit the whole of it, some will be confined to the south-western counties, some will be shared with other parts of Great Britain.

The 'social acceptability' of dialect varies according to region, and my impression is that today West-country dialects stand rather low in popular esteem. We may note also the different attitudes a person may have towards his way of speech. Some glory in the local vernacular, while for others it is a cross to bear, or at the last a disadvantage to be overcome, leading to timidity in speech, a real sense of inferiority and a feeling of envy for the 'well spoken', although they may only be speakers of a more acceptable dialect, e.g. Cockneys. The desire for correct speech leads to mistakes such as the addition of h to such words as arm, or up. This is over-correction and may give rise to problems of understanding. If the word *where* has to be pronounced with the sound [ɛ] and not [ɜ], i.e. similar to 'were', should not *shirt* be pronounced 'shert' [ʃɛrt] or *skirt* as 'skert' [skɛrt]. Add a short vowel between the [r] and the [t] of skirt and we end up with skerret [skɛrət] (rhyming with ferret) and the puzzle is complete. Yet this is the pronunciation of which at least one Edwardian young lady was very proud. The acquisition of R.P., or at least an acceptable pronunciation, by a child from a dialect-speaking home can be a difficult and confusing process. When I was at school well-meaning teachers were horrified at what to us were familiar turns of phrase, and I remember a remark made in the playground about an aeroplane '*Igh, en er*?' ('high, isn't it?') reproduced in the school magazine under the title 'English As She Is Spoke'.

This leads us to another aspect of dialect, that is its social significance. If we hear someone speaking dialect, we can often tell from which region he comes and we recognise him as a member of the 'lower classes', and in this we are largely correct. Investigators generally choose people of little education as their informants. As noted above a rise in the status of a family often meant the acquisition of R.P., at least by the children. However, the position seems to be changing in two ways; more and more people are speaking modified R.P., that is with a limited number of dialect characteristics, an 'accent' for instance, and more of these modified forms are becoming more acceptable.

Dialect and R.S. are not the only forms of English. Dialect uses many of the elements of both R.S. and of colloquial English. The aim of this book is to describe the dialects of the south-western counties, that is the way they differ from R.S. or commonly accepted colloquial English. The three main areas of language study are phonetics, grammar and vocabulary—the sounds, the forms of words and sentences, and the words themselves. These will form the main sections of the book.

2 THE PHONETIC ALPHABET

When we study language we must carefully distinguish between the spoken and the written forms, that is between the sounds and the letters used to represent them when we write. Our alphabet came to us via the Roman missionaries who converted the Anglo-Saxons. It had had a long history even before the Romans adopted it, so it cannot be said to be 'tailor-made' for our language, as, for example, the Kyrillic alphabet was for the Slavonic languages. In fact the letters only roughly indicate the sounds they purport to represent. If an Englishman is asked how many vowels there are in English, he will probably save five—A, E, I, O and U. Yet if we construct as many words as possible beginning with h and ending with d with a vowel sound in between, we get *hid, heed, head, had, hod, hood, hied, hoed, hard, hear* and *hoard*, and we easily see that there are more than five vowel sounds. In the same way, there are more consonant sounds than letters. To enable our alphabet to cope with the extra sounds we often use two letters to indicate one sound, e.g. sh in *ship*, but not always in a particularly logical manner. Ea represents one sound in *meat*, another in *head*, while in *read* it may be either.

Received Standard is as much a written form of language as it is a spoken form and if we were writing a book on it we could use words in their ordinary spelling, confident our readers would know the pronunciation. Dialect has no standard written form and all writers have found it necessary in some way to indicate the pronunciation. In the nineteenth century ordinary letters were often used, examples of which will be found in the opening chapter. The practice led to some rather strange statements such as 'A is always pronounced as R' (*Monthly Magazine*, 1814).

Linguists, conscious of the need to indicate the sounds of speech in writing, have developed a special system of notation, called the International Phonetic Alphabet or I.P.A. for short. This consists of a large number of symbols, each representing one sound; for instance [ʃ] represents the first sound in *ship* for which we use sh in ordinary spelling. Some use will be made of I.P.A. in this book, so a short account and a reference list follows.

Vowels
Vowels are sounds that can be the centre of syllables. The basic sound

for all vowels is made with our vocal cords, but this is modified in various ways by such means as opening the mouth more or less, rounding the lips or raising the back, middle or front of the tongue towards the roof of the mouth. This latter is the most significant factor.

In the following list, the tongue is raised and held relatively steady. (Phonetic symbols and an example of a word containing the sound in R.P. are given.)

[i]	heed	[ɪ]	hid	[ɛ]	head
[æ]	had	[ɑ]	hard	[ɒ]	hod
[ɔ]	hoard	[v]	hood	[ʌ]	bud
[u]	rude	[ɜ]	heard	[ə]	perhaps

(In *perhaps* the symbol refers to the first vowel sound.)

In some vowels, the tongue is not held steady, but moves as the sound is produced, giving a double vowel, or diphthong. These have two symbols.

[aj]	tie	[ou]	home	[ej]	lay
[ɔj]	boy	[au]	how		

There are more complicated dipthongs which are produced by our rather unusual [r] sound, in such words as *lyre* or *hear*, but as this sound will need a good deal of explanation in later chapters, it need not detain us here.

The consonant sounds and symbols present fewer problems [p] [b] [d] [t] [f] [v] [k] [g] [s] [z] [w] [n] [m] [h] stand for the sounds they normally represent. In addition we must use:

[ʃ]	for the sh sound in *ship*	[ʃip]
[ʒ]	for the g sound in *rouge*	[ruʒ]
[tʃ]	for the ch sound in *chip*	[tʃɪp]
[dʒ]	for the j sound in *jam*	[dʒæm]
[ŋ]	for the ng sound in *sing*	[sɪŋ]
[θ]	for the th sound in *thin*	[θɪn]
[ð]	for the th sound in *this*	[ðɪs]
[j]	for the y sound in *yes*	[jɛs]

[l] stands for the first sound in *lamb*, where the tongue touches the roof of the mouth, but there is another l sound, often heard in *field*, where the

13

tongue remains in the bottom of the mouth, the so-called 'dark' l, represented by the symbol [ɫ].

[r] represents the first sound in *ring*, but more will have to be said about r later.

With the help of these symbols, we can give an accurate account of dialect pronunciation.

3 PRONUNCIATION

The pronunciation of the dialects must first be described, as it is, perhaps, the most fundamental aspect of our study and it will explain many points when we come to consider grammar and vocabulary.

Human beings are capable of producing hundreds of different sounds. Of this large number, each language chooses about 40 or 50—R.P., it is said, has 45—to the exclusion of the others. Different languages do not necessarily use the same sounds, as those who learn foreign languages know. Some sounds are used frequently, some rarely; for example, the g sound in 'rouge' [ʒ] is heard only in a few words, borrowed from French. Most can occur in any position in a word, but a small number are restricted to one place; e.g. the ng sound, which, in English, is only used at the end of a word.

Sounds are divided into vowels and consonants. Vowels form the centre or nucleus of a syllable, and, in addition to the traditional list, we must add [n] and [l] (in such words as *rotten* and *little*).

One fairly new idea in modern linguistics is that of the **phoneme**. Phonemes are sounds which distinguish words. *Tea* and *sea* are different words, so [t] and [s] are different phonemes. But in *tree* the [t] is pronounced rather like a ch sound. This special kind of [t] is only used before [r] so it does not contrast with the ordinary [t] sound, which never occurs in that position. So these may be different sounds, but they are the same phoneme. The phoneme system of a language is very important, as it is a major factor in our understanding of the spoken word.

Some sound-changes in dialect cross phoneme boundaries. For instance, *pig* is often pronounced [pɛg], like 'peg' which is quite another word in R.P. Equally *peg* can be pronounced [pæg], rhyming with 'bag'. Much work still needs to be done to establish what system of phoneme contrasts each dialect uses, and in this book I shall note the differences between dialect and R.P.

People sometimes speak of a west-country 'burr'. This recognises the importance of the [r] sound in the dialects of our area. We must first consider the position of the [r] sound in R.P. Our English [r] is not the strongly trilled Scottish [r], where the tongue taps against the back of the teeth, nor the guttural French [r], where the back of the tongue is raised and rasps against the uvula (the little 'stalactite' that can be seen at the back of the mouth). It is a rather weak combination of these two, the tip

15

of the tongue being raised towards the teeth, but not touching them, and the back of the tongue being raised towards the uvula but not constricting the passage of air to the same degree as in French. This sound was much more widespread in the sixteenth century, but since then it has disappeared in the final position or before a consonant in words that are still spelled with an r. Today at the end of such a word as *lower*, the tongue just falls limply into the botton of the mouth, producing a [ə] vowel sound. In this way we have acquired a new range of diphthongs in words like *board*, *hare*, *bier* or *poor* ([ɔə], [ɛə], [iə], [və]). In *car* the r indicates the value of the vowel, but is not pronounced at all.

In the south-western dialects, the [r] is slightly different. The tongue is raised a little higher both back and front and is much more tense than in R.P. More importantly, it is pronounced before consonants and in the final position. When final it may be preceded by an [ə] sound. In this way [r] has given rise to diphthongs in dialect as it did in R.P., but it did not disappear in the process. As an example we may take the word *floor*, [flɔ] in R.P. In dialect the word is pronounced [vluər].

The [r] sound may also 'colour' vowels. One very important element in the production of a vowel is the raising of a part of the tongue towards the top of the mouth. When [r] follows, the highest point moves a little further back. In the word *carry* the vowel in dialect is similar to that of 'car' in R.P., i.e. [kari] not [kæri]. When we deal with consonants there will be even more to say about [r].

We can now consider the simple vowels used in dialect. These are where the tongue is raised and held relatively steady. Of the vowels of R.P. [i] [ɛ] [jɒ] [ʊ] and [ə] are much the same in dialect. In [ɪ] [æ] [ʌ] the highest point of the tongue is further back giving a rather different value to the sound. In the vowels associated with [r], i.e. [ɑ] in *hard* and [ɜ] in *heard*, the same movement occurs, giving, with the [r] the characteristic 'burr'. [ɔ] is often replaced by the diphthong [uə]. [u] is used as in R.P. in most of our area, but in west Somerset, Devon and east Cornwall it has been fronted (that is the highest point of the tongue is nearer the teeth), to give the well known [Y] sound as in *school* or *do*.

It is not easy to describe pronunciation, and we are lucky today to have such easy recordings facilities, giving us, we hope, permanent examples of dialect speech even if dialect speakers disappear. However, such methods are relatively expensive and not always readily accessible, so we may have to resort to other means, simple description as in the last paragraph, or a vowel diagram. This is a conventionalised cross section of the mouth as seen from the left side, on which is plotted for each vowel

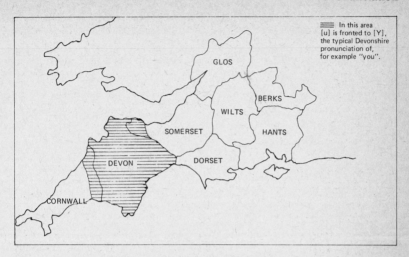

the highest point of the tongue. (As stated in the last chapter, the most significant factor in the production of vowels is the raising of the back, middle or front of the tongue more or less towards the roof of the mouth.) In the following diagram vowels in R.P. are shown as o, those in dialect as x.

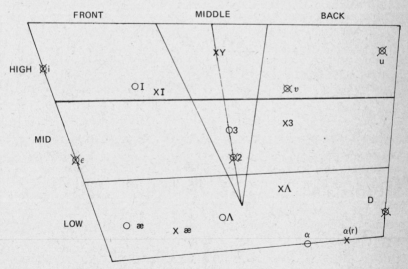

We now come to diphthongs. These are vowels where the vocal organs—the tongue and the lips—move as the sound is being produced.

17

As was seen in the last chapter there are five diphthongs in R.P., excluding those caused by a following r. They are longer than simple vowels, but in dialect even simple vowels tend to be long and, in a number of cases, they have segmented, that is broken up into two distinct sounds, thus making a *diphthong*. One example is the word *ash*, pronounced [æjʃ], the first part being similar to the sound in R.P. and followed by a y sound [j]. Another is *tart* (sharp, as used of pain), which is said as [tiərt] that is the sound begins with the vowel in 'heed' [i], then the short [ɑ], and, of course the r.

In R.P., all diphthongs are 'falling', which means that the first element bears the stress. If we try to lengthen inordinately the vowel in, for example, *lay* (i.e. [lej]), we say e-e-e-j, not e-j-j-j. Falling diphthongs are usual in dialect, but the position can reverse, 'rising' diphthongs being produced. *Meat* is often pronounced rather like 'mate' [mejt], but is also heard as 'myet' [mjɛt], a rising diphthong. *Home* is sometimes [uəm], but the [u] is often shortened to [w] and the [ə] lengthened to [ʌ] (as in bud), giving the pronunciation [wʌm]. (The word 'one' in R.S. is a southern dialect form which developed in a similar way. Had the east-midland form prevailed, as it did in the majority of cases, we should have said [oʊn] and this accounts for the strange spelling.)

Diphthongs are much less stable than simple vowels, and even in R.P. there is much variation in the pronunciation of words such as 'I' or 'no'. (Think of the caricatures of certain types of people that appear on the stage or on television—the Colonel, the Don, the Duchess, the shop assistant—and the ways in which they might pronounce these words in their exaggerated accents.) In dialect there is also a good deal of variation, usually in the way the first element is pronounced, though, as just noted, in changing to a rising diphthong as well. The following is a list of variations that, in addition to the usual value, are heard in south-west England. In the rest of the book, I shall refer to each group by the value it has in R.P.—the one at the head of the list, but it must be assumed that any of the other forms can take its place. The reader might like to try to pronounce each of these with the aid of the reference table given in chapter 2.

[aj] as in *mine*. [ɒj], [æj], [əj], [ʌj], [ɔj]. (This last is the 'Oi' in *Oi be a varmer's boy* in that most fictitious of dialects, Mummerzet.) In west Somerset, Devon and east Cornwall [æ], [a] and [ɑ] are heard. This is because of a tendency to 'fronting' in the area (giving in the case of [u] the sound [Y]), that is moving the highest part of the tongue forward, and in the diphthong the [j] has been absorbed by the first element.

[ej] as in *gate*. [aj], [æj], [əj], [ɛj], [iə], also [jɛ] as a rising dipthong.

[ɔj] as in *join*. [ɒj], [aj], [ɑj], [æj] [ʌj]. In Wiltshire, Dorset, Hampshire and Gloucestershire, there is strong tendency for a [p] or [b] to produce a [w] in front of this diphthong, *boy* being pronounced 'bwoy' (e.g. [bwɔj]). *Boil* and *poison* are other examples, as well as the dialect word *pine*, a cowshed.

[oʊ] as in *load*. [ɔʊ], [oə], [u], [uə], [ɔə] and in its rising form, in such words as *oak*, *oats*, *home* or *coat* [wɒ], [wæ], [wə], [wɪ], [wo], [wʌ], [wʊ]. In *going* the effect is rather as if it rhymed with 'swine'.

[aʊ] as in *hour*. [æʊ], [ɒʊ], [əʊ], [ʌʊ], [ɔʊ], [ɛʊ]. In west Somerset, Devon and east Cornwall, where [Y] is prevalent [æY], [əY], [ɑY] are heard.

It will be noticed that there is certain amount of overlapping between the various diphthongs.

We must now list the sound changes which cross the phoneme boundaries, i.e. those that use a 'different vowel sound'. Once again the keynote is variety and a word may appear in more than one group. *Egg*, for instance, can be pronounced as [ɪg], [æg] or [ɛjg], that is rhyming with 'big', 'bag', or 'vague'. These changes affect individual words, not all words containing the vowel. *Keep* is often pronounced [kɪp], but *meat* cannot be said as [mɪt]. In the following section the change and the pronunciation of a key word are given in phonetic script, but to help those who find this difficult, an approximate indication of the change is added in ordinary letters. Some examples are given, but the list is not necessarily exhaustive, and notes on distribution or other features of interest have been added as needed.

1) [ɪ] > [ɛ], e.g. [pɪg] > [pɛg] (*pig* sounds like peg). A fair number of words—*milk, drink, big, dig*. Also common in the negative forms of the verb is, e.g. [ɛʒnt] or [tɛnt] or [tjɛnt], *is not* or *it is not*.

2) [i] > [ɪ], e.g. [lik] > [lɪk] (*leek* sounds like lick). Found in many common words—*keep, week, needle, sheep, been*. The other word 'leak' never has this change. Also verb forms such as *thee nis'n* [ði nɪsn], *thou needest not*, and in the past tense of *to see* [zɪd], i.e. *see-ed*. This sound change accounts for a common misconception about an English saying, 'to spoil a ship for a ha'porth of tar'. The likely victim is a sheep and the tar was to be put into the sheep-dip to rid the fleece of parasites. A ha'porth of tar would not go very far on a ship.

3) [ɪ] > [ʌ], e.g. [rɪdʒ] > [rʌdʒ] (*ridge* rhymes with fudge). Only found in this word and *bristles*, as far as I rhyme, but it explains more radical alterations to such words as *riddle* > *rudder* (sieve), or *brittle* > *bruckly*.

4) [i] > [ɛ], e.g. [hit] > [hɛt] (*heat* rhymes with let). A few words only—*cheap, heat*. Somerset, Wiltshire, Dorset and counties westward.

5) [i] > [ej], e.g. [ki] > [kej] (*key* sounds like kay). A fair number of words have this sound change—*cream, clean, reach, meat, these, tea*. In the case of *tea*, this an archaic pronunciation, once acceptable in highest circles. Alexander Pope wrote of the Queen:

And thou, great Anna, whom three realms obey,
Doth sometimes counsel take, and sometimes tea.

Meat is also pronounced [mjɛt] and *bean* is usually [bjɛn]. A few other words can have this rising diphthong as well.

6) [ɛ] > [ʒ], e.g. [wɛr] > [wɜr] (*where* sounds like were). *Herrings, buried, hare, hair, merry, terrible, errand*.

7) [ɛ] > [ɪ], e.g. [dɛf] > [dɪf] (*deaf* rhymes with stiff). A number of words including *bellows* (in its double plural form, [bɪləsɪz]), *pension, bread, egg, breast, yesterday* and *yes*. In Somerset, Devon and Cornwall *deaf* is heard as [dif], rhyming with reef, and a few other words have this vowel change.

8) [ɛ] > [æ], e.g. [bɛg] > [bæg] (*beg* sounds like bag). A large number of words are affected, including *egg, yellow, leg, sweat, sexton*. We may also put on this group the word *waistcoat* in its formerly acceptable, but now colloquial pronunciation of [weskɪt], which becomes [wæskɪt].

9) [ɛ] > [ej], e.g. [hɛd] > [hejd] (*head* rhymes with aid). *Egg, leg* appear here again. *Chair, dairy* have a [ə] sound before the [r] i.e. [tʃejər]. Only a few words involved.

10) [ɛr] > [iər], e.g. [ʃɛr] > [ʃiər] (*share* rhymes with pier). *Care, spare* and *scare*.

11) [æ] > [ej], e.g. [græs] > [grejs] (*grass* rhymes with race). In addition

to *ash, father* and *rather*, the negative forms *can't* [kejnt], and *shan't* [ʃejnt].

12) [æ] > [ɛ], e.g. [kætʃ] > [kɛtʃ] (*catch* sounds like the surname of the famous hangman, Jack Ketch). A few words, *axle, thatch,* and *can't.*

13) [æ] > [ɒ], e.g. [ræp] > [rɒp] (*wrap* rhymes with top). A few words including *sat, rat* and *apples.*

14) [æ] > [ɑ], e.g. [kæri] > kɑri (*carry* has the same vowel as car). *Marry, carrot, barrel*—due to the influence of the following [r].

15) [ar] > [iər], e.g. [tɑrt] > [tiərt] (*tart* has the same vowel sound as fear). *Cart, spar, garden, smart.*

16) [ɒ] > [æ], e.g. [drɒp] > [dræp] (*drop* rhymes with trap). A few words—*fog, trolley.* Also in *wasp,* but this is probably a survival of an older pronunciation of words beginning with [w].

17) [ɑ] > [ɔ], e.g. [dog] > [dɔg] (*dog* has the same vowel as daw in jackdaw). A few words—*cross, off, dog, cloth.* This is also a survival of an earlier acceptable pronunciation, and one which can still be heard from some speakers who pride themselves on the correctness of their speech. In addition the word *wash* [wɔʃ], which is also pronounced with [aj] as its vowel [wajʃ].

18) [ɒ] > [ʌ], e.g. [dɒg] > [dʌg] (*dog* sounds like dug). *Frog, donkey, tongs.* West Somerset and Devon only.

19) [ɔr] > [ar], e.g. [kɔrn] > [karn] (*corn* rhymes with barn). Many words in which we have [ɔ] followed by [r] and a consonant—*morning, corner, lord, forty, north* to give but a few examples. This is an interesting sound change from the point of view of distribution. It appears in west Hampshire and west Berkshire, is general in Wiltshire, Gloucestershire and Dorsetshire, and also in east Somerset, but disappears in west Somerset and in the whole of Devon, but reappears briefly in Cornwall.

20) [ɔ]. Words like *floor, roar, more,* etc., are heard with a variety of vowels—[o] [u] [ɔ], often with a [ə] before the [r]. The pronunciation of floor [vlʊər], rather like the vowel in 'poor' is perhaps the most typical.

Wessex Dialect

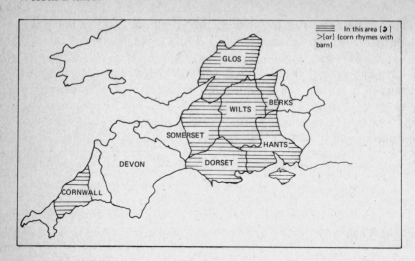

In this area [ɔ] >[ɑr] (corn rhymes with barn)

21) [ɔ] > [aʊ], e.g. [pɔr] > [paʊr] (*pour* sounds like power). *Four, story* and a few others.

22) [ɔ] > [æ], e.g. [sɔs] > [sæs] (*sauce* rhymes with mass). *Straw, all, claw, daughter* and *law,* especially in *mother (in) law.* Sometimes words such as *claw* or *bawl* have the vowel [ej] as in lay.

23) [u] > [ʊ], e.g. [rut] > [rʊt] (*root* rhymes with put). *Soon, afternoon, soup, whooping (cough), shoot, roof, hoof, soot.*

24) [u] > [ʌ], e.g. [huf] > [hʌf] (*hoof* rhymes with puff). *Boots, brook, roof.* Somerset, Wiltshire and Hampshire only.

25) [ʌ] > [ɪ], e.g. [sʌtʃ] > [sɪtʃ] (*such* rhymes with rich). *Mother, Sunday, brush, dozen.* Very common in Devon.

26) [ʌ] > [aʊ] e.g. [dʌst] > [daʊst] (*dust* sounds like dowsed). *Ruts, crust* and also *shovel* (v not pronounced [ʃaʊt]). One age-old and international children's rhyme is the request to the snail to come out of its shell. The west-country version of it runs as follows:

Snail, snail, come out thee house,
And I'll gie thee a barley crust.

This sounds change is necessary to get the rhyme.

27) [ʌ] > [ɛ] e.g. [skʌl] > [skɛl] (*skull* rhymes with sell). *Plunge, shove, shut*—only a small number of words and in Wiltshire and Gloucestershire.

28) [ər] > [ɑr]. These are the 'Derby/Darby' words. Two hundred years ago there was much uncertainty about how to pronounce words containing -er, but now R.S. has agreed upon one pronunciation or another—[ɑr] in *clerk* and [ər] in *certain*. American usage does not always correspond to English. Dialect differs from R.P. in such words as *learn, certain, worms* and *fern*.

We now come to three sound changes which we may describe, rather unscientifically I fear, as 'dropping the r'.

29) [ar] > [æ], e.g. [parsən] > [pæsən] (the first syllable in *parson* has the same vowel as mass). *Parcel* also.

30) [ɜr] > [ʌ], e.g. [kɜrs] > [kʌs] (*curse* rhymes with fuss). *Worse, worst, purse, first, furze*—not unknown in colloquial English as is shown by the rhyme:

Thrice armed is he whose cause is just,
But four-times armed who gets his blow in fust.

31) [ɔr] > [ɒ], e.g. [hɔrs] > [hɒs] (*horse* rhymes with boss). The only other example I know is *morsel*. In Anglo-Saxon the r could shift its position in a word, as it still can in south-western dialects (see later on in this chapter 'metathesis'). So the older Anglo-Saxon form 'hross' became 'hors'. This may account for this change, of sound, which is perhaps the word 'hross', simplified by dropping the r.

32) [ə] disappears at the beginning of a word such as *enough*, pronounced as 'nuff' [nʌf]. *About, abide another.*

33) [ə] is inserted between consonants as in *elm*, ellum [ɛləm]. Our ninteenth-century predecessors called this change 'svarabhakti'—opening out, a word from a now dead language of India, Sanskrit. It reminds us that Sanskrit grammarians were among the first to study the way they spoke in the fourth century B.C. and that they produced what H. A. Gleason, the American linguist, considers to be the most sucessful and complete description of a language ever made. *Skirt* [skɛrət], *film* [fɪləm] and *worts* [wɛrəts] are other examples.

Wessex Dialect

Real sound changes in diphthongs present fewer problems, but we must remember what has already been said about the number of varieties of each.

34) [ej] > [æ], e.g. [bejbi] > [bæbi] (*baby* rhymes with tabby). In *acorn, acre, apron* and *hate* the sound is [jæ] and may be the result of a rising diphthong.

35) [oʊ] > [u], e.g. [loʊd] > [lud] (*load* sounds like lewd). *Go, hose, bone*. Often this sound is [uə] as in toad [tuəd] or post [puəst].

36) [oʊ] > [ɒ], e.g. [noʊ] > [nɒ] (*know* sounds like gnaw). *Post, snow, clothes, close, road*. In west Wiltshire, sentences are liberally interspersed with 'dost know' pronounced [snɒ], as in 'That ent right, sno''.

37) [oʊ] > [ə], e.g. [ʃædoʊ] > [ʃædə] (*shadow* rhymes with adder). *Furrow, Marrow, Window*. Occasionally this -ow ending can become [-i], in minnow [mɪni] or winnow [wɪni].

We now come to consonants. Consonant changes have so far been left out in order to concentrate on the vowels, but of course a dialect word may be subject to two, three or even more changes, before we arrive at the usual form. However, consonants are more clear-cut, and there is less overlapping between categories. Once again it must be said that these changes affect individual words only, not all the words containing the consonant in question.

The first kind of change we shall deal with is, perhaps, the one that typifies and, so far as it is possible, delimits the south-western dialects. This is voicing of consonants, usually at the beginning of a word. We use our vocal cords to produce all of our vowels, but only some of our consonants. When we do so, we produce 'voiced' consonants; when we do not, but rely on the hiss of passing air, we produce 'unvoiced' consonants. In English there are pairs of consonants, made in much the same way as far as the position of the lips and tongue is concerned, but one voiced and one unvoiced. These pairs are [p]/[b], [f]/[v], [s]/[z], [t]/[d], [θ]/[ð] and [ʃ]/[ʒ]. Voicing is using the second of these instead of the first [z] for [s], etc. It is heard in west Hampshire, west Berkshire, south Gloucestershire, throughout Wiltshire and Dorsetshire and in Somersetshire, except for a small area around the Mendips, but it is most frequent in Devon. In Cornwall, it disappears towards the west of the

24

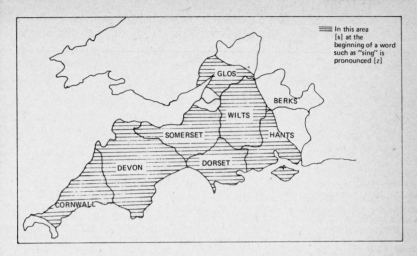

In this area [s] at the beginning of a word such as "sing" is pronounced [z]

county. The details are as follows:

38) [f] > [v] in *feet, fiy, fox, floor* and almost all words beginning with [f]. In the middle of words or at the end as in *loaf*, voicing is confined to west Somerset and Devon. The word *vixen* is a south-western form that has become standard, the initial [v] hiding the fact that it is closely related to 'fox'.

39) [s] > [z] in *saddle, sack, cider*. Almost universal when [s] precedes a vowel, but rarer in words where [s] is followed by a consonant, e.g. *small* or *stubble*.

40) [θ] > [ð], that is the th as in *thin* is replaced by the th as in *this*, in words such as *thistle, thatch, thigh*. In Devon only we hear the sound in *mouth*—the noun; in R.P., with this pronunciation, it is a verb, so in dialect the distinction between verb and noun disappears.

41) [ʃ] > [ʒ], *shepherd* is pronounced as 'zhepherd'. It is difficult to give any indication apart from the phonetic alphabet, as the [ʒ] sound is rare in English. Heard in words like *shilling, sure*, etc.

42) [t] > [d]. Rather different from the previous changes as it never affects the initial consonant, but is heard in *water, kettle* and similar words.

Another almost as typical feature of the south-western dialects is the omission of [t] or [d] at the end of a word when either of them follows another consonant.

43) [t] > — in *harvest* [ɑrvɪs], *slept* [slɛp], *kept* [kɛp] as also shortened forms of *not*, e.g. *had'n, weren't* pronounced [wɛrdn].

44) [d] > — in *field* [vɪɫ], *rind* [rajn], *end* [ɛn] etc.

Before a vowel [t] or [d] are maintained, as in 'the end of the road', [ðɛnd ə ðə rɔd].

Next we have to look at another phenomenon, **metathesis.** This the shifting of consonants in words. One good example is:

45) [æsk] > [æks] (*ask* is pronounced like axe). This double form of ask goes back as far as Anglo-Saxon, 'ascian' and 'axian' being alternative infinitives. *Pixie* with its Devon and Cornish form pisky is a similar change.

46) [sp] > [ps] in words like *hasp, clasp* or *wasp*, giving haps, claps and wops.

But the consonant which is subject to metathesis most consistently is [r]. The Leeds Dialect Survey found that *hundred* was pronounced *hunderd* in all but three cases in the south-west. Many examples could be given but a few must suffice—run, [ɜrn], brush [bɜrʃ], children [tʃɪldɜrn] and dialect words such as rudder (a sieve), which becomes *herder*. This last exemplifies another fact, that where [r] was at the beginning before it changed its position, an [h] may be added as [hɜrn] for run. The usual change is for an [r] to move from before a vowel to behind it, but in a few cases the reverse takes place, *curds* becomes cridds and *curdle*, criddle. Metathesis of r was common in Anglo-Saxon and, once again, there were two parallel infinitives for the verb *to run*, 'rinnan' and 'iernan'. Not all words have a metathesised form. Grass, for instance, is never changed, although the word in Anglo-Saxon could be gærs, and this still exists in the place-name Garston (grass enclosure). So we list as sound change number.

47) Metathesis of [r].

Assimilation has already been mentioned. This is when the movements of the lips and tongue run into each other as when:

48) [n] > [m] in *oven* [ʌvm] and similar words (*seven, eleven*). This is not the end of the story, however, as a further assimilation takes place. To make a [v] we have to put the lower lip against the top teeth, but to make an [m] the lips are put together. We miss out the first movement and put the lips together straight after the vowel thus getting [ʌbm], [sɛbm] and [əlɛbm], the usual pronunciations. *Devon* is sometimes spelled 'Deb'n' in rhymes on picture post cards. Another case of assimilation is *tidn* for *it is not*.

49) Excrescent [t] or [d]. These are extra consonants put in a word, either through inexact use of speech organs, or through misapprehension of the correct form in a basically illiterate society. Nineteenth-century writers give numerous examples, such as *cavaltry* (cavalry), *carnder* (corner) and a large number of comparative adjectives, e.g. *tallder* (taller). As far as I know, I have ever heard or used only one example of these in *werdn'* for *were not*, so possibly the second of the explanations given above is correct and widespread literacy has caused this feature to all but disappear.

Next we come to two pairs of changes of which one is the reverse of the other.

50) [k] > [t] (*bleak* is pronounced as bleat). *Ask* is another example.

51) [t] > [k] (*bleat* is pronounced as bleak). *Pant, mist, sleet* and *mast* (beech nuts) are said as pank, misk, sleek and mask.

52) [s] > [ʃ] (*suit* is pronounced as shoot). *Susan, slice, suet*, and *sukey* (i.e. a diminutive of Susan and used as 'black sukey', a kettle).

53) [ʃ] > [s]s (*shrink* is said as srink). *Shrivel* and the dialect word *shrammed* (very cold) are other examples.

The last two are confined to the eastern counties of our area.

It will have been noticed that in the vowel section there have been several reverse pairs [ɪ] > [ɛ], [ɛ] > [ɪ], [ɛ] > [æ], [æ] > [ɛ], [æ] > [ɒ], [ɒ] > [æ]. It seems likely that these sound changes were made in certain words, perhaps having in them a historical origin, were transferred by analogy to other words with the same sound, then the process of correction set in and was in its turn extended to other words that had not been mispronounced in the first place, ending in a certain amount of confusion over which was the correct form and which was not. Once again, it must be said that many dialect speakers had little or no acquaintance with written English and therefore had no reference point as to correctness.

54) Omission of consonants. A few miscellaneous examples: [b] in *chamber* [tʃɪmər]; [ð] in *with* [wi], *without* [wiaʊt] and *scythe*; [f] in *after* [ætər]; [v] in *give* [gi], *serve* [zɑr], and *shovel* [ʃɛʊt]; [n] in *kiln* [kɨl] and *iron* [ajr]. One case must be given a section to itself.

55) Omission of [w] before [ʊ] and [ə] (*wood* is pronounced [ʊd]. An important and widespread feature, extending north-eastwards well beyond the counties we are concerned with. *Wool, woman, awkward* and *athwart* are other examples, and also *would*. In the family name *Woodward* the change takes place twice. The reverse is also occasionally found and [w] added to *whooping* (*cough*) and to *whole*.

56) Various changes with [θ] or [ð]. [θ] becomes [d] before [r], (a 'retracted' d, rather the first sound in jam, used in R.P. *dry*) in words such as *three* [dri], *through* [dru] or throw [drɒ]. [θ] becomes an ordinary [d] in an area centred around Devon in *thatch* and *thistle*. In a wider area it may be [v] in the same words. [ð] becomes [d] in *farthing* and *further*.

57) [d] > [t] at the end of words such as errand, orchard or second, [ɜrənt], [artʃət], [sɛkənt].

Much has been said in the section on vowels about rising diphthongs beginning with [j]. Some cases are not at all clear-cut and a few more words here will not be amiss. *Gate* is pronounced yat [jæt] in Wiltshire and Gloucestershire. Many words having an initial [h] in R.P. have [j] in dialect, e.g. *hate* [jæt], *herrings* [jɜrɪnz], *head* [jɛd] or *heat* [jet]. Some may be explained as rising diphthongs but not all. The insertion of [j] after a consonant, as in gander [gjændər] or carrots [kjærəts] is mainly found in Gloucestershire but is also heard in other parts of the south-west.

The word *with* needs a section on its own. It is often pronounced 'be' [bi]. This has led to its being confused with 'by' in sentences such as *I 't 'n bi a 'ammer*, but that this cannot be the case is proved by 'Come along with I' [kʌm lɒm bi aj]. Note the assimilation in *along*.

Dialect shares with ordinary colloquial English many features which purists condemn as 'slovenly'. [t] > [ʔ]—the glottal stop, in the middle or at the end of words. This sound, although widespread, is associated with cockney speech, as in bu'er. It is made in the throat, not in the front of the mouth. [θ] > [f] in *breath* or *thumb* etc.; [ð] > [v] in *breathe*. Three others deserve fuller treatment.

One is the use of the 'dark' ł, which is often heard before a consonant or at the end of a word, as, for example in 'field'. Bristolians are noted for adding a [l] to all words ending in a [ə]; thus *idea* becomes ideal [ajdiəł], *America* becomes Americal etc. Perhaps this explains the name of their city. Originally it was Bristow—the *bridge place* (stow = place)— so the final l is etymologically incorrect.

The ending of the present participle is -in not -ing, and other words ending in -ing have the same change, except those of one syllable. The dialect speaker is constantly using the -ng sound but chooses to use the other form with longer words. The present participle in Anglo-Saxon ended in -ende, this being the origin of the -in ending which has been transferred to words such as morning, but not to monosyllables as these cannot be confused with participles.

The last feature we must refer to is the dropping of [h]. This is widespread in dialect and always has been in my experience—even in people who were old when I was a child and who learned to speak in the 1850s. I therefore doubt certain statements made by nineteenth-century writers. In Goddard and Dartnell's *Glossary of Wiltshire Words* published by the English Dialect Society in 1893, it is said that 'the cockney misuse of H is essentially foreign to our dialect. Formerly it was the rarest thing to hear a true Wiltshire rustic make such a slip, though townsfolk were by no means blameless in this respect'. A letter from the Rev. G. Hill supports this view; 'I should like to bear out what you say with regard to the use of the letter h in South-West Wilts. When I lived in these parts twenty years ago, its omission was not I think frequent. The putting it where it ought not to be did not I think exist. I find now that the h is invariably dropped, and occasionally added, the latter habit being that of the better educated.' This seems to me to be wishful thinking, a nostalgia for the past (note that in both quotations the position is very different today), allied with the idea that countryfolk are somehow 'pure' and townsfolk 'corrupt'. The first of the passages cited above continues with a lament that 'the spread of education and the increased facilities of communication have tainted even our rural speech with cockneyisms and slang phrases'. In a Life of St Edith, written at Wilton in the fifteenth century such spellings as hit (it), hende (end), or hevensong with ʒere (here, ʒ = y) show that uncertainty about h goes back a long way. Wishful thinking is not unusual in dialect studies, especially among those who like to attribute great antiquity to the local vernacular, calling it 'the living speech of our Anglo-Saxon forefathers' or some equally imaginative description.

One part of dialect pronunciation has received little attention, if any. This is intonation, the rise and fall of the voice as the sentence is unfolded. It plays a very important part in our understanding of what is said, marking the end of sentences, for instance. In English we use four tones, three for our ordinary speech and the highest in times of stress. At the end of a statement we rise to the third highest and then fall to the lowest, at the end of certain questions we leave the sentence as it were unfinished by staying on the third highest. The second is the normal tone. My impression, for what it is worth, is that dialect uses basically the same patterns of intonation as R.P., but the high notes seem higher and the stressed syllables longer. In the sentence 'I do put a bit of fertiliser on 'em' the syllable fer- is very high and very long before the voice descends for the end of what is said.

This chapter deals with the form of words and the ways in which they can be combined into sentences. A very traditional form of grammar used to be taught in schools, and in some cases still is. However, this subject has received much attention from linguists in the present century and many new and important ideas have been evolved. On the whole I shall adhere to traditional school grammar in this chapter, with one or two exceptions.

In traditional grammar, the first word in 'The book is on the table' is an article, but the first of 'My book is on the table' is an adjective, although it is obvious that they both perform the same function—as a 'noun introducer'. In this book all such words—my, our, this that, etc.—are listed under articles. In traditional grammar, nouns are divided into four categories—common, proper, abstract and collective. A further division of common nouns into **Mass** and **Count** nouns explains a good deal both in English and in dialect grammar. Mass nouns are names of substances like butter, flesh or bread. Count nouns are names of individual objects such as pencil, cat or apple. With this distinction we can make such statements as 'Mass nouns have no plural', 'A and an are used only with count nouns' or 'Some is used with the singular of mass nouns and the plural of count nouns'. (This latter is a useful test of whether a noun is mass or count.) Some nouns can be used both as count and mass, usually with a change of meaning, slight, as 'a potato/some potatoes' compared with 'some potato', or considerable, as in 'an iron' compared with 'some iron'. This distinction will be used to explain some points of dialect grammar.

Articles

THE DEFINITE ARTICLE (the): The pronunciation 'thee' [ði] before a vowel is rare. It is either pronounced as normal, or the vowel is elided so that *the end* is heard as th'end. It is used much the same as in R.S., except that it comes before names of ailments—one has 'the chicken pox', 'the rheumatics' etc.—and with the word 'both', e.g. 'I'll take the both on 'em'.

THE INDEFINITE ARTICLE (a or an): *An* is rarely used, *a* coming before a vowel, e.g. 'I got a apple'. The *a* is usually run so close to the following word that it is not heard, but the intention to say it is there and if the speaker were asked to repeat slowly he would definitely include it. One

usage not found in R.S. is before a number as in 'about a fifty of them'.
DEMONSTRATIVES (this, that, these, those): *This* is reduced to *'s* in front
of the two words 'morning' and 'afternoon' as in *'smornin'*. In other cases
the position is rather complicated. *This*, pronounced 'these' [ðiz] or
'thase' [ðejz], and *thick* [ðɪk] do duty for 'this'. *Thick* and *thuck* [ðʌk]
(Gloucestershire, north-east Wiltshire and Hampshire) as well as *thicky*
in Devon correspond to 'that'. It will be seen that *thick* can be used for
either, often in the same area, and by the same speaker. However the distinction is not critical. French manages very well with only one
demonstrative *ce*. The only time when the difference is important is when
there are two objects in question. Then French attaches -ci or -là to the
noun and, in the same way we can add *here* or *there* to the
demonstrative, 'this here house' or 'thick there tree'. So far as we have
been talking about count nouns. With mass nouns *this here* and *that
there* are used, 'this here flour' or 'that there soup'. In the plural, *these* is
pronounced as 'thase' [ðejz], but *those* is replaced by 'they' or 'them',
'these here apples' and 'they beds' or 'them birds' being examples of ordinary usage.
POSSESSIVES (my, your, his, its etc.): Until not many years ago, *my* was
said as 'me' [mi] when unstressed, and on the London stage, Hamlet
could be heard saying 'Oh, me prophetic soul'. In dialect, we still say 'me'
or 'thee', instead of my or thy, except when we have to make a distinction
between, say, 'thy brother' and 'his brother'. *Its* is not used, *his* or *her*
replacing it. (More will be said about gender of words, and how pronouns
replace them under the section PRONOUNS). Our is used for close
relations as in 'our mother' or 'our John'.
AR AND NAR: These are two of the most interesting features of dialect.
The most likely origin of these words is that they are shortened forms of
'ever a' and 'never a', but even if it is so, the way in which they are used
has gone far beyond any associated word or phrase in R.S., and they
have become what amounts to an interrogative and a negative indefinite
article, no parallel to which exists in standard English. They are used
with count nouns as in 'Got ar match?' or 'I ain't got nar spade' (double
negatives are common in dialect), compared with 'I got a dog'.

Nouns
POSSESSION: The indication of possession by *of* or its variant *on* is more
common in dialect than in R.S., as 'the father on 'un' instead of 'his
father' or 'the sill of the window' for 'the window sill'. However
apostrophe *'s* is used and may be appended to a phrase as well as a noun,

for example 'the woman who works in the factory's daughter'.

PLURALS: The old plurals, ending in -en instead of -s are rarely heard now. The Leeds Dialect Survey noted *housen* in Berkshire and Gloucestershire, but nineteenth-century investigators found many more examples—*wenchen, wopsen* (wasps), *cheesen, peasen*, etc. The Cunnington Manuscript (see bibliography) says that these plurals were almost universal in north Wiltshire 200 years ago. I am reminded of the shepherd who, not too long ago, when asked how they separated two flocks of sheep which had got mixed up, replied 'We do look at their veasen (faces)'. Another variant plural concerns words which end in -st; in these words -es, pronounced [ɪz] is added, giving *beastes, postes, ghostes* and *nestes*.

Double Plurals are those where the plural form is, mistakenly, construed as a singular, and a second plural ending is added. An example in R.S. is *children*, the original plural being *childer*, and *-n* was appended—the old plural suffix. In dialect we have *bellowses*, pronounced [bɪləsɪz]. Other examples are *beasteses, posteses* and *hameses*. (Hames are part of the harness of a draught horse, but is used, jocularly to mean braces, to keep the trousers up, or as they are more commonly known in the south-west *bracers*). Elworthy, in his account of the dialect of west Somersetshire, tells of a sign he saw in Exeter in 1850, which contained two double plurals. It read:

> *Here liv'th a man who don't refuse*
> *To mend*
> *Umbrellases, bellowses, boots and shoes.*

Some words do not change for the plural. In some areas *woman* is one of these. They are more commonly names of measures, 'six year ago', 'five mile back' or 'ten foot tall' being normal. The last is, of course acceptable in R.S., but the alternative, 'ten feet tall' is rare in dialect. Other measures which do not add a plural ending are *rood* (= ¼ acre), *rod, perch* and their dialect equivalent *lug* (= 30¼ sq. yds.), *pound* and all weights greater than a pound. *Acre, ounce, inch, yard, hour, day* and *week* add -s as usual.

Broth is considered plural in Somerset and one can speak of 'a few Broth'. *Way* often has an -s in 'a little ways further on'.

Adjectives

R.S. has an adjectival ending -en meaning 'made of' as in wooden and golden. This ending is much more common in dialect. One can speak of a 'dirten floor', a 'stuffen gown', a 'bricken bridge', 'wheaten straw' or, with

33

a rather different signification 'boughten bread'. The stairs can be the 'timbern hill'. *Glassen*, too, exists and a local character with well-worn trousers was known as Joey Glassenbreeches. *-en* is added to dialect words, such as Devonshire *cloam*, earthenware—'a cloamen pot'.

Endings may also be added to other adjectives, as *rounden* or *fitty*.

COMPARISON: Comparatives are formed in English either by adding -er (one syllabled adjectives or those ending in -y) or by using 'more' (e.g. bigger, heavier but more intelligent). Dialect makes more use of the first method as, e.g., *beautifuller*. Double comparatives are also found, *more dearer*. In Somerset, an excrescent d was often introduced into a comparative as *tallder* or *fullder*. Much of this applies to superlatives. We find *beautifullest*, double superlatives, *most commonest* and Somerset superlatives such as *talldest*.

Shakespeare used double superlatives—'the most stillest night' and a letter in a recent daily paper deplored the bad grammar of the Book of Common Prayer in which 'most highest' appears.

Pronouns

The use of pronouns is one of the most characteristic features of southwestern dialects, but the overall picture is very complicated. One of my earliest expeditions into dialect studies was discussing with a friend from Devonshire whether 'She's looking at we' was more correct than 'Er's looking at us'. The second person singular—i.e. *thou* and *thee* in R.S.—is still much used in our area, mainly between intimates. The pronouns *I, thee, he, she, we, you,* and *they* are used when there is a need for emphasis, no matter what function it has in the sentence, whether it is subject or object. Apart from these uses, the position is summarised in the following table, but it will be necessary to expand the information in notes appended at the foot. We must take three categories, subject of a statement, subject of a question (including 'tag' questions, the 'have you', 'can't I' or 'did they'? of R.S.) and object pronouns.

	SUBJ. STATEMENT	SUBJ. QUESTION	OBJECT
1st pers. sing.	I[1]	I/us	I/us/me
2nd pers. sing.	thee	(thee)[5]	thee/ee
3rd pers. sing. masc.	he/'a[2]	er	'n
fem.	she/er[3]	she/er	er/she
neut.	he/she/'a/it[4]	'n/er/it	'n/er

1st pers. plur.	we/us	we/us	we/us
2nd pers. plur.	you	ee[6]	ee
3rd pers. plur.	they	em[7]	em

NOTES:

1 In a small area of Somerset, called by A. J. Ellis 'the Land of Utch', and defined by him as 'the angular space between the two railways which have their vertex at Yeovil, Sm., on the border of Dorset', at least until a few years ago, if not at present, the old pronoun ich could be heard as in *'chill*, I will or *'cham*, I am.

2 Stressed form *he*, unstressed *'a*.

3 In Somerset, Wiltshire, Berkshire and Dorset there is a strong preference for *she*, whether subject or object, although *er* is used occasionally, especially with 'be'. In Devon, Cornwall and Gloucestershire *er* is almost universal. The distribution of *we* and *us* is much the same.

4 *It* is used to replace mass nouns and in the indefinite sense, i.e. 'What time is it?' *It* is shortened to *'t* in *'tis*, *'twas* or *'twere*. I think that the form *'tis* was the dialect feature that persisted longer than any other in my attempts to grapple with R.P. When a pronoun is needed to replace a neuter count noun, e.g. box or the name of an animal, a form of *he* or *she* is used. In the latter case the obvious one is not always chosen, *he* being sometimes used to refer to a cow. When talking of inanimate objects I find it natural to say *he* and my impression is that *she* is less common. In Hampshire it is said that everything is *he* except a tom cat. More thoughtful people say this is a gross exaggeration, pointing out that a waggon, a carriage and a saw may also be referred to as 'she'.

5 In questions the subject *thee* is usually left out, as in *Cas'n see as well as thee couldst, cast?* (Your excellent vision has somewhat deteriorated, has it not?). The verb-form tells us which subject is intended. Leaving out the subject is unknown in R.S., but is common in languages which have verb endings such as Latin.

6 *ee* is perhaps a form of 'ye'. If so this is the reverse of the way it is used in the Authorised Version of the Bible where 'ye' was the subject and 'you' the object 'Blessed are ye when men shall revile you ...'.

7 *em* is not a 'slovenly' form of 'them', but the Old English pronoun 'heom'. It will be noticed that there are a number of similarities between the last two columns of the table. Presumably there was a certain amount of confusion over pronouns which followed verbs whether as the subject of a question or as a direct object.

Pronouns are also used with the imperative ('commands'), as in 'Do ee have a drop more', or 'Thee mind thy own business'.

Now we come to the pronouns *arn* and *narn*. These are related to the articles *ar* and *nar*. The stressed forms are *ar one* and *nar one*. They are used like the articles, *arn* in a question 'Have you got arn left?', *narn* in a negative statement, 'You want a spade, but I ain't got narn'. They also have a sense akin to that of 'either' or 'neither', e.g. 'You can have arn of they three kittens' or 'I had six apples yesterday and now I ain't got narn left'.

POSSESSIVE PRONOUNS: (mine, yours, his, etc.). Dialect has mine and thine, but continues the series with *hisn, hern, ourn, yourn* and *theirn*. It is thought that these were formed by analogy with mine and thine, but I was always under the impression, for what reason I do not know, that they were shortened forms of his own, etc. Thus the cautionary verse

> *He that takes what isn't hisn*
> *When he's caught he's sent to prison*

rhymes in dialect, not in ordinary English.

RELATIVE PRONOUNS: (who, which that). Dialect brings in *as* and *what*, the latter usually replacing 'which' and even 'who'. *Whom* is never heard, nor is *whose* which is replaced by such turns of phrase as 'The man what his house burnt down'. In R.S. the relative pronoun can be left out when it is the object of the verb in the relative clause, e.g. 'The car I bought was dud'. In dialect we can also omit the pronoun when it is the subject of the following verb as in 'There's somebody at the door wants to see you'. The preposition always comes at the end. 'This is the key what I opened the door wi'.'

INTERROGATIVE PRONOUNS: (The same pronouns as above, basically, but used to ask questions.) The usage here follows Standard English much more closely. *Who* always refers to persons, *what* to things. *Whose* is used, but not *whom*. *Which one* has an unstressed form *which 'un*.

DEMONSTRATIVE PRONOUNS: (This, this one, that, that one, these and those). *This,* pronounced as normal [ðɪs] for mass nouns, 'If that milk ain't no good, have some of this', *this one*, pronounced this 'un for count nouns. *That* and *thick 'un* follow the same pattern. In the plural, *they* is common, 'Gie I two o' they'. *Them* is also used especially as the antecedent of a relative 'Them as did it'. *These-um* is a form of these.

REFLEXIVE PRONOUNS: (myself, etc.). In line with what was said about the pronunciation of my and thy, *meself* is usually pronounced 'myself' [mɪsɛlf] and *thyself,* 'theeself'. *Hisself* replaces 'himself', and *theirselves* 'themselves'.

STRESSING PRONOUNS: (As above but with a rather different use, e.g. 'I made it myself'.) All that was said under Reflexive Pronouns applies here.

Adverbs

This is a rather vague category into which are put all those words which do not fit in easily elsewhere, so, even in grammars of R.S., we find a whole variety of different usages.

Dialect uses other adjective intensifiers (very, etc.), e.g. *main, tarblish* (terriblish) or *real*. 'I do feel main bad'.

In common with vernaculars all over England, adjectives and adverbs have the same form, e.g. 'he do talk beautiful', said of someone who had recently acquired a pseudo-cockney accent.

In comparisons, the first *as* is often left out as in 'He's daft as an adder', or replaced by so, 'so quick as lightning'.

Than is always reduced to *'n*—'He's bigger 'n I'.

Verbs

In English we shorten so many words that we use with verbs—*I'll* for 'I will' or 'I shall', *we'd* for 'we had' or 'we would' or *they've* for 'they have'—that when we write them out in full, they tend to look cold and stilted, which is why so many writers prefer the short forms. There is an even greater air of unreality when dialect verbs are committed to print.

As stated under PRONOUNS, the second person singular is in common use, *thee* being the usual subject pronoun, rather than *thou*, as in R.S. THE INFINITIVE: (This is the form of the verb used with 'to', e.g. 'I want *to go*', or which follows an auxiliary verb such as *can, must* or, and this is most important in south-western dialects, *do* e.g. 'I can *play*' or 'do you *know?*'). One of the most interesting features of speech in our area is the existence of the so-called 'free infinitive'. This was a special form of the verb which ended in -y, pronounced [i], e.g. *makey* for make. It is little heard now, but was common in the last century. Writers then had a certain amount of difficulty in explaining its use, but the one I have found most helpful, F. Elworthy, said it was used intransitively, that is when the verb has no direct object. Thus, 'I do dig the garden', but 'Every day, I do diggy for three hours'. Even then it was dropped before a vowel. The prevalence of 'do' forms meant it was frequently heard. The quotation illustrating the free infinitive in the Cunnington manuscript is, I think, worth including in its entirety: 'Well Mary, how do you get on in Life? what do you & your family do now to get a living in these times-Wy zur we do all vind zummut to do—Jan, ye know, he do Smithey (work as a smith) Jin the beggist wench do spinney the Little one do Lace makey—I do Chorey (go out as a Chore Woman) and the two Boys do Bird keepey—that is One works as a smith—one spins one makes Lace one goes out as a Chore woman & two are Birdkeepers which Latter term were more to the purpose if expressed Bird frightener or driver'.

This is presumably the last trace of the Anglo-Saxon infinitive which ended in -ian. The Leeds Survey found only the occasional example of its use, but dialect turns up in many strange places. As I was writing this chapter, I saw a review of a science-fiction play, broadcast on B.B.C. 2 on 15 March 1978, concerning a future world where the population was divided between the agricultural and the industrial workers. The title of the play was 'Stargazy in Zummerland'. *Stargazy* is evidently a free infinitive.

Another feature we may note here is the pronunciation of the verbs 'empty' as *empt* or 'carry' as *carr*. This is probably a case of over-correction, taking off a -y that was a part of the word, not the free infinitive ending.

But the matter goes farther than that. We find 'quarry' as *quar,* and 'minnow' which is sometimes changed to 'minny' turns up as *min*. Other words ending in -ow which lose their final syllable are 'farrow' and 'furrow', probably through a sequence such as -ow > -y > —. Thus words which are not verbs are corrected in this way. However, the adjective *empty* is never changed.

THE PRESENT PARTICIPLE: (the -ing form of the verb). This can also have the -y of the free infinitive as in 'They be going a-courtyin''. Notice also the a- that comes before the participle.

THE PRESENT TENSE: the verb 'to be'. This, as in most languages, is the most complicated, having several alternative forms which when joined with the number of possible pronouns give a great variety of expressions.

> *I be*
> *thee bist/thou art* (the latter in parts of Somerset)
> *he's/he be/'a's*
> *she's/she be/'er be/'er's*
> *it be/'tis* (also as for he and she: see pronouns)
> *we be/we'm/us be*
> *you be/you'm*
> *they be/they'm*

In the negative, apart from *thee bisn't, ent* or *ben't* are used, with all subjects the last being pronounced often as [bjɛnt], or in Gloucestershire as [bjʊnt]. In questions *be* is generally used although *is he* and *is she* are alternatives, and we must say *bist thee*.

OTHER VERBS. In English we have two present tenses, the continuous, e.g.

'I am reading', and the frequentative, e.g. 'I read'. Continuous tenses are formed as in R.S., except that all the varied forms of the verb 'to be' are used—*I be digging, thee bist going, we'm leaving*, etc. These tenses are comparative newcomers in English and the dialect speaker may occasionally prefer the other form of the present tense. 'Do rain, don't it?' he might remark, glancing out of the window, instead of the more usual 'It's raining isn't it?'.

Frequentative tenses in dialect are of two distinct kinds. There is the one formed with the auxiliary verb 'do', as in 'I do see 'e every day', and the other where -s is added to all persons of the verb, e.g. 'I goes there often'.

'Do' forms: These, of course exist in R.S., but are used to emphasise, to ask questions or when the sentence is negative. People who are not accustomed to dialect often feel that a great fuss is being made with all the 'do's' about things of no importance. 'Do' never changes, even for *he* or *she* and is pronounced [də] or d' before a vowel. Shakespeare often uses these forms and actors invariably use the R.P. pronunciation of 'do'. I think it would be nearer his intention if they followed dialect usage.

'-s' forms: It is possible to add -s to most persons of the verb, but is usual with 'they'. The old eth ending of the 3rd. person singular can still be heard occasionally in Devonshire and Cornwall.

The stronghold of the 'do' forms is Dorsetshire but they are also found in Wiltshire (especially the western half), in Somerset and in parts of Gloucestershire. Devon prefers the -s form with 'they' but the other reappears briefly in west Cornwall.

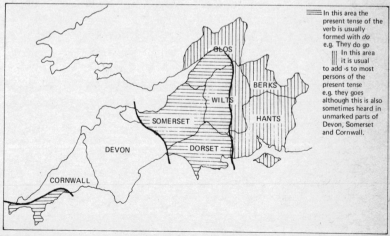

In this area the present tense of the verb is usually formed with *do* e.g. They do go

In this area it is usual to add -s to most persons of the present tense e.g. they goes although this is also sometimes heard in unmarked parts of Devon, Somerset and Cornwall.

Wessex Dialect

FUTURE TENSE: Much the same as in R.S., the tense expressing a mixture of futurity, intention and obligation. When using it for the last of these we find very occasionally a stressed form of shall [ʃɒl]. The question form of wilt (thou) is *'oot* [ʊt]. ''oot do it?', and in the negative 'oosn—'oosn do it, then?'

THE PERFECT TENSE: In dialect this tense is sometimes made in much the same way as in R.S., except that we usually say *he've* and *she've*. There is, however, another form as exemplified in 'He bin a-gid I a shilling'. The *a* before *gid* may well be a remnant of old Anglo-Saxon prefix ge- which became i- in Middle English, before it disappeared in R.S.

PAST TENSES AND PAST PARTICIPLES: Classifying past tenses is quite difficult in R.S. On the whole they are divided into three categories:

1) Strong verbs, where the past is indicated by a change of vowel, e.g. *tread/trod, shake/shook.*

2) Weak verbs, which form their past tense by adding the ending -ed, e.g. *look/looked, walk/walked.*

3) Mixed verbs where there is a vowel change and also an ending is added, e.g. *feel/felt, bring/brought.*

The past participle is usually the same as the past tense, although a number of strong verbs have *-en* added to a form, which may be the present, e.g. *fall/fallen*, or the past e.g. *froze/frozen*, or with a different stem, e.g. *drive/drove/driven.*

In dialect verbs do not necessarily belong to the same category as in R.S. The following is a list of the changes that are found.

a) Weak or mixed verbs in R.S. that are strong in dialect: examples *creep/crope, scrape/scrope.*

b) Strong verbs in R.S. which are weak in dialect: examples *see/see-ed* [zɪd], *give/gi(v)ed*. There is a large number of such verbs—*blow, drink, know, dig, hurt, kneel*, etc.

c) Verbs that add an ending to a strong form: examples *steal/stoled, take/tooked*. In *bornded* there are at least two past endings.

d) Verbs with a different strong form from R.S.: examples *slit/slat, (a)bide/(a)bid.*

Dialect makes little difference between past tenses and past participles.

e) Verbs, the past participles of which are used as past tenses: Examples begin/begun, come/come, e.g. 'I begun yesterday'.

f) Verbs the past tenses of which are used as the past participles: Examples speak/spoke, bite/bit, break/broke, e.g. 'I've spoke to 'an already'.

There is a frequentative past tense formed with *did*, parallel to the *do* present tense as in 'Every day we did fetch the milk', the existence of which is ignored by every book on dialect which I have consulted.

In the verb 'to be' both *was* and *were* can be used for all subjects except 'thou'. In the negative *were* takes an excrescent d, 'werdn't', quite often. With 'thou' or rather its south-western counterpart 'thee', *wast* or *wert* are the usual forms, but in the negative we say *wersn' thee*.

OTHER TENSES: In *shouldn't have, can't have* and similar verbs *have* is reduced to 'a [ə]. In *ought to have* 'to have' is expressed by the same sound, e.g. 'You ought 'a found 'en'. ('You ought to have found it'.)

Numbers and Times

Some older people still use numbers like *four and twenty*. This is relatively common in times—*five-and-twenty past,* or *five-and-twenty to. Half after* is often heard instead of 'half past'.

Prepositions

OF and ON: J. Kjederqvist remarks in his *Dialect of Pewsey*, 'In M(iddle) E(nglish) the two prepositions 'of' and 'on' could both have the weak form a . . ., and having thus encroached upon each other's dominion of pronunciation, they also encroached upon each other's dominion of signification'. As he goes on to show this is a considerable simplification of the real situation. *Of* never replaces 'on', but *on* occurs in places where we might have expected 'of', mainly in front of the unstressed pronouns *'en* (him), *it* and *'em* (them). For the rest *of* is used, pronounced o' [ə] before a consonant, and of [əv] before a vowel. In this section when we speak of 'of', the use of 'on' as detailed here is implied.

'OTIOSE' OF: This is *of* used before the direct object of a verb, as in *I be stackin' on 'em up*. Much more widely found formerly, it is now confined to sentences where the pronouns 'en, it, and 'em are the objects. This use only occurs with continuous tenses, i.e. the *am/was/shall be doing* type and formerly when nouns followed the *of*, a- usually preceded the participle as in *I were a-peeling of the potatoes*.

IN LAW: The *in* is omitted from these relationships, e.g. *brother law* etc.

WITH: 'Accompanied by' is expressed by *along of* or *along with* the latter being pronounced [lɒm bi]. *Along of* means in addition 'because of'—*Twere all along o' you that I had to go*.

OTHER PREPOSITIONS: The dialect speaker is not usually satisfied with 'to' or 'at'. He may use one for the other as *I be living to Taunton* (one of Elworthy's examples), but on the whole, he prefers to use *up, down* or *over*. *Over* is the preposition suitable for nearby towns and villages, *down* is in the general direction of Land's End and *up* in the opposite direction. Thus in West Wiltshire we say 'up Swindon' and 'down Plymouth', both for going and being there, but in Cornwall, everywhere beyond the Tamar is *up-country*. Other, less expressive prepositions may need reinforcing, as 'up in town'. In a similar way *off* is almost always followed by *of*, as in 'I knocked 'un off of the table'.

We must now consider the words used in the south-west. To many people, local words form the essence of dialect and a book about dialect should, according to them, be a long list of unusual words. To a linguist, however, vocabulary is the least satisfactory aspect of dialect, as words are elusive and changing all the time. Sound changes are a much better basis for a framework of dialect study.

Let us take some examples to indicate the difficulties of defining a dialect word. *Tree* is of course used, its pronunciation and meaning being the same as in R.P. In *farmer* [vɑrmər] we have a word the pronunciation of which is unmistakably west-country, but recognisable by any English speaker. Now the word *zar* or *zarrin* [zɑr, zɑrən] as in *I be going to zar the pigs*, or *Gie I another girt zarrin o' that pudden*. If we apply sound changes 28, 39, and 54 we find this is simply the word 'serve' or 'serving'. Such a word (especially as *zar* is used in a different sense from 'serve' in R.S.) is not immediately recognisable by a non-dialect speaker. The compilers of several nineteenth-century vocabularies got it right, but it led the editors of the Leeds Dialect Survey to postulate a word 'sarrow' to feed. (Such mistakes are easy to make. There may well be some in this book. One word which was deleted at the last minute was one I received from a Wiltshire shepherd—*vierdn* for fern. I associated it with words as 'verdant' or 'verdure' but realised eventually that it is simply a variant pronunciation of the word 'fern' itself.)

When we see a word such as *bruckly* surely we have found a dialect word. But no, *bruckly* is 'brittle', once again explained by sound changes 3 and 51, and with an adjectival ending. 'Brickle' was once an acceptable alternative and is found in the Authorised Version of the Bible—Wisdom XV 13, 'This man that of earthly matter maketh brickle vessels'. Where do we draw the line that divides dialect words from ordinary English words? This is an important question when compiling a dialect vocabulary and the choice may well have to be arbitrary.

Words, too, may be used in a different sense in dialect. *Rough* is used to mean 'ill', *brave* to mean the opposite, 'well', *Parson* can be used of non-conformist ministers. Normal English words may be compounded and take on a quite different meaning, e.g. *back-friend*—an agnail (rough skin at the base of a finger nail).

In R.S. each word has one spelling and when said in isolation, usually one pronunciation (though considerable variants are heard in actual speech, determined by adjacent sounds cf. 'brem butter'). The spelling gives an unchanging standard. In dialect, however, we are often confronted not with words, but with word-clusters. Goosegrass is called variously in the south-west *clide, cliders, clites, cly* and *clivers*, all linked with a widespread name 'cleavers'. Convolvulus has such names as *withwine, withywine, withywind, withwind* and *willowind* as well as *beddywind, bethwine, bettywind, bedwine, beswine* and *bedbind*. These groups are obviously variants of the same word—but which is the original?

Another difficulty is the presentation of dialect words. As noted in previous chapters, no conventional spelling exists as it does in R.S. Strictly speaking, the words should be listed in the phonetic alphabet, but that would be tedious for all but the dedicated specialist. The Leeds Survey gives its finding in phonetics, but at the head of each section summarises the answers in ordinary spelling. The writer of a book on dialect often has to invent spellings for the words he uses and then the un-phonetic nature of the English alphabet becomes a handicap. Do we spell [dʒɪbɫz] (onions) *gibbles* or *jibbles?* Is [lɪər] (empty, hungry) spelt *lear* like the King or *leer* like the look?

In any case what is the correct form of a dialect word? We have seen how dialect sounds vary from those of R.S. These rules for changes often apply to dialect words, only this time we are not sure which is the standard form of the word. Urine collected from public houses and workhouses and used in Wiltshire for scouring cloth was known as *seg* although some people said *sig*. Or was it known as *sig* although some people said *seg*. Is the verb to frighten *galler* or *gally*, or shall we use the version Shakespeare used and list it as *gallow?*

We have spoken of the variety of forms of one word. Another aspect of the variety of dialect is the number of words used for one idea. The classic example is the word for a weakling pig. Those used in our area are; *cady, dack, dallpig, dilling, darling, darrel, dorrel, joey, little joe, rinnick, runt, squeaker* and a whole group beginning *nestle* or *nuzzle* and ending *-draf, -drish, -drudge, -bird* and the most common *-tripe* (e.g. nestle-tripe). Haws—berries on the hawthorn—have a large number of different words, *aglons, eggles, hawberries, mayberries, egglets, eglons, hags, hagags, pigberries, pighales* and *pigshells*. 'Left-handed' is also well represented; we find *back-, cam-, gammy-, keck-, keggy-, marlborough-, scram-, scrammy-, skivvy-, squivver-, watty-, click-, clicky-, skiffy-, coochy-, scoochy-, squiffy-* and *squippy-handed* in the south-west.

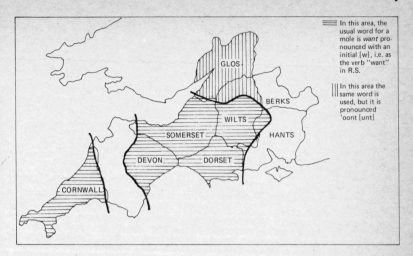

In this area, the usual word for a mole is *want* pronounced with an initial [w], i.e. as the verb "want" in R.S.

In this area the same word is used, but it is pronounced 'oont [unt]

GLOS·

BERKS

WILTS

SOMERSET

HANTS

DEVON

DORSET

CORNWALL

Words are used, too, in areas of differing size, some being found in the whole of the south-west and even beyond, some restricted to one locality. We belong to that part of England, nearly half of it, where it is more usual to talk of *ricks* rather than *stacks*. *Mow* has the same meaning but is only current in Devon, Cornwall, Somerset and Gloucestershire. *Blind House*, a lock-up, refers to 11 such places on the Wiltshire/Somerset border. My grandmother always spoke of something small rather contemptuously as 'a little firk', I have not been able to find any trace of this word in reference books, not even the English Dialect Dictionary, so it may have been a word used only by our family.

The English Dialect Dictionary, spoken of above, consists of six large volumes and must contain thousands of entries. Consulting it, one is sometimes surprised at finding that what one had assumed to be a 'real west-country word' is in use in a large part of England—*sloom*, to dawdle, does not feature in any of the localised vocabularies published by the English Dialect Society but is of wide currency according to the E.D.D. On the other hand words and expressions which one has grown up with, realising eventually that they are not standard English, do not appear. Such for me was *firk* mentioned above, and several others.

Where do all these words come from? The historical study of languages is a matter for specialists. Each word needs an investigation of its own to establish its ancestry, Anglo-Saxon and Middle English texts need to be searched to find related forms and corroboration sought in Germanic and other Indo-European languages. A detailed etymology for each word is outside the scope of this book, but I shall occasionally refer to the history of some of the entries in the vocabulary. Here we shall look in general terms at the origin of dialect words.

It was stated at the beginning of this book that English is a Germanic language, and some words remind us clearly of their counterparts in German. *Lear*, meaning 'empty' or 'hungry' is obviously German 'leer' and the usual west-country form of the literary 'thou art' is similar to 'du bist', *thee bist*. Many dialect words are survivals from Anglo-Saxon or Middle English which have dropped out of the standard language. *Emmet*, an ant, was used by Chaucer and around the year 1600 Michael Drayton wrote in his 'Nimphidia':

> *At length this lover did devise*
> *A bracelet made of emmets' eyes.*

Want has been replaced by 'mole', *frore* by 'frozen', *pig-lewze* by 'pig sty' and *barm* by 'yeast'. These are but a few examples of words now obsolete in R.S., but still used in dialect.

The words quoted above would not be understood by a non-dialect speaker, but one of them, *emmet* is merely a variant of the normal word 'ant'. The Anglo-Saxon 'æmete' gave rise to both, but one was eventually rejected by the standard language and the other retained. The rejected form is preserved in dialect. Another, more complicated case is *evet* a 'newt' (literary 'eft'). 'An evet' became 'an ewt' and by mistaken division 'a newt'. Mistakes of this kind are not unknown. 'An adder' is from 'a nadder' and 'an apron' is the French word 'napperon'. In dialect we find *nole* for 'hole' and *ettle* for 'nettle'.

Dialect words have their origin in other languages beside Anglo-Saxon. The Danes stayed only briefly in Wessex before their defeat at Ethandune, and it is not to be expected that they influenced speech as much as they did in Northern England, except in so far as these changes became generalised in standard English (e.g. replacement of the Anglo-Saxon pronoun 'hie' by the Scandinavian 'they'). However, the borrowing of certain features from northern dialects can explain the form of some words in the south-west. One of the hallmarks of these dialects is the use of *k* where in the south we have *ch*, e.g. *kirk* = church. Thus a pair of words such as 'dyke' and 'ditch' are cognate, that is they are both derived from the same word, the first a northern, the second a southern form. Both belong to standard English, with related, but different meanings. *Dyke* is used in a very special sense in the south-west, or at least a part of it, as 'a lavatory'—originally an earth closet. A word of definite Scandinavian origin and of widespread use, but in my experience confined to children, is *jonnick*, 'honest'. Another, rather more puzzling, is dialect *flick* or *fleck* related to 'flitch' a side of bacon. This last word is not used in our area and would be, I think, relatively unknown were it not for the 'Dunmow flitch'. The dialect words certainly do not have that meaning, but are used for the 'caul' fat that comes from around a pig's kidneys and that is used to wrap faggots in, or any fat from a pig. Conversely to all this we find in dialect characteristically southern forms with ch where the word in standard English has k, e.g. *blatch,* 'black', *hunch* 'hunk' and *smeech* 'smoke'.

Latin has also left its mark. In Somerset a form used to address a number of people, such as, for example, a farmer speaking to his workmen was *soce*, from Latin 'socius', an ally; this is possibly a remnant of the language used by preaching friars in the Middle ages. 'Nolens-volens', unwilling-willing is also found, usually corrupted to *nolus-bolus* or *vorus-norus*, pronounced [vɑrs nɑrəs]. It is said to mean 'willy-nilly', but the only use I know for it is in the phrase 'a girt vorus-norus wench', where it means 'wilful' or 'brazen'. 'Gemini', twins, as in the sign of the Zodiac, is an expression of surprise and has various forms, *jimminy* being one.

French supplies some words. *Croupy*, to crouch is French 's'accroupir, accroupi'. This word can also be *coupy* (sound changes 29–31). 'Abattre' is thought to be the origin of the word *batter*—'a slope of a wall, a kind of buttress to shore up old buildings'. It is a technical term in architecture, but is used in dialect for the railway embankments. In the old day of steam trains, the *batters* were frequently on fire. When we hear of a personal tragedy, we can say 'I be main sorry for 'ee'. *Main* is the old French 'maint', now used only in 'maintes fois', many times. The dialect word corresponds to 'very' but we must notice that 'a very few people' means a small number, while 'a main few people' means a large number.

Cornish, the old language spoken in the west of the county until some 200 years ago, has now died out, but some of its words have passed into dialect. *Bucca*, 'a scarecrow', *muryan*, 'an ant' and (*pig's*)-*crow*, 'a pigsty' are examples.

Some words retain meanings that they have lost in standard English. In *The Winter's Tale*, when the shepherd finds the baby he says 'A boy or a child, I wonder?'. Here a 'child' meant, not a young human of either sex, but a girl. This signification is still attached in some dialects. 'Girl' is not a common word in any case, *maid* or *wench* being usual in its place. In the standard language 'maid' has been specialised into a servant and 'wench' is now used only as a joke. The dialect word *drang, drong, drung* means a passageway between buildings, but it is the same word as 'throng'. The noun in English now means 'a crowd', but the verb retains in it some idea of movement. Distinctions may be made by individuals that are not recognised in English, or even by the remainder of dialect speakers, as when a farmer, needing a new hand, advertised 'Strong lad or chap required'.

Longer and more unusual words have always presented problems to the dialect speaker and the result of his efforts to master them have often been a distortion of the original. 'Rheumatism' is always *the rheumatics, lattyprack* is said to be 'paralytic', Elworthy quotes *aumligus* for 'omnibus' and *willygog* represents 'whirligig', a turnstile in the original sense and then a roundabout at a fair. On my father's allotment grew little pansy-like flowers, which we called *love-a-lidos*, but which were really 'love-in-idleness'. Whether we can take all these distortions seriously I take leave to doubt. The dialect speaker has always been able to vary the tone of his speech and does this often to obtain a joking atmosphere: the broader the dialect, the greater the joke. I suspect that some of these forms were arrived at as part of a big joke.

In the north-eastern part of our area the word 'to retch' is *keck* but in other localities *urge* is used. This is obviously retch with a metathesised r, but the final sound is altered because of the other word 'urge', to egg on. This process, by which one word causes a change in another is known as CONTAMINATION. When a vase or a china object breaks, it is said to be in *flitters* or in *flittereens*, this last because of the influence of 'smithereens'. Another local expression is 'a pair of trucks', just one of those hand barrows that roadmen and decorators used to push around before the war, but still used in 'a pair of sack trucks'. A stranger, who moved into the area, being told by the removal man that he would have to get a pair of trucks to shift an especially heavy piece of furniture, waited in great expectation to see such a feat of skill, where one man used two barrows at the same time, only to be disappointed when one turned up. It seems that these very useful aids were formerly called 'a pair of wheels' and the present expression is a combination of that phrase and the word 'truck'.

Some words are given prefixes or suffixes that are different from the ones used in R.S., such as *-ful* in 'mischieful or *-some* in 'blundersome', or that are really superfluous as *unthaw* which simply means 'thaw', or *unempt* which some dialect speakers reserve for 'unload', rather than just 'empty'. We have already noted the fact that extra endings may be added on to adjectives, as *roundy, steepy, fitty* or *wetty*. In the south-west 'raisins' are known as *figs* and the favourite pudding made with them is 'figgy duff' or with a longer ending 'figgety duff'. Most dialects, it seems, have a preference for words that begin with *s*, and often add this letter to words that begin in some other way. 'Crunch' becomes *scrunch*, 'whittle', *squittle* and 'plash', *splash*. These are called 'sibillated' words and one finds that the **S** section of a dialect dictionary or vocabulary is always longer than any other. The reverse also applies, there is over-correction and words that should begin with s lose their first sound as quat for *squat* as 'Quat (sit) down there'.

There is a law in Semantics—the science of meaning—which states that the amount of meaning attached to a word varies in inverse proportion to its frequency. In other words, the commoner the word, the less it conveys and the rarer the word the more it conveys. We can easily see this in 'The cat sat on the mat', 'the' which is used in every other sentence we produce tells us very little (something like 'the aforesaid'), 'sat' and 'on' are of medium frequency and tell us more than 'the' and the meaning 'peaks' (forgive the jargon) in 'cat' and 'mat'. We can apply this rule to figurative expressions too. If I hear 'So-and-so is as strong as an ox', no image of a bovine slips into my brain. I treat 'as an ox' in as cavalier a fashion as I might 'very' if I had heard 'So-and-so is very strong'. This and similar phrases are part of our everyday language and are unfairly stigmatised as 'clichés'. If, every time we wanted to speak of a person's strength, we found ourselves obliged to think up a new simile—in other words if we sought after originality in speech—we should tire ourselves and our listener by the effort involved. 'As an ox', when speaking of strength does its job admirably, without any unnecessary intrusion into our train of thought. We should remember, and teach our children, that language is a tool that has a workaday task to perform, and is only rarely a medium of artistic expression, and then preferably in expert hands.

Non-dialect speakers, when they come across a dialect metaphor, attribute to it an originality—an 'earthiness' or a 'pithiness' are favourite descriptions—which, in fact, they do not have. I think no more of saying in dialect 'I be so cold as a frog' than I do of saying 'I'm as cold as ice' in R.P. This is not to say that dialect speakers are incapable of being original, but the majority, the vast majority of our metaphorical expressions are borrowed from speaker to speaker, as indeed they are in R.S. If we must have a phrase that will conjure up our sturdy forefathers in their struggle with Nature to provide a living for them and their families, independent yeomen, jack blunt and as much a part of the landscape as the earth from which they sprang, and in which their bones will rest, what better than—'as strong as an ox'.

With this in mind we may now give what can be a representative list of this kind of expression in dialect. Those which refer to a defect in another person predominate. All are given in the normal English form, but it must be remembered that 'as' at the beginning can be left out or changed to 'so' in dialect.

> as bald as a bladder
> an egg
> a plate
> as blind as a beetle (a hammer; see in the vocabulary).
> as cold as a frog
> as clean as a daisy
> a pink
> as daft as a bat
> a (scrubbing) brush
> a donkey
> a monkey
> a mule
> an owl
> a pig
> as deaf as an adder
> a broom
> a dish
> a door
> a haddock
> as dirty as the pot
> as drunk as a sack
> as dry (thirsty) as a fish
> as easy as pit-pat-pan
> as fat as a want (mole)
> as giddy(-headed) as a goat
> a ram
> as glad as a bird
> as hairy as a badger
> as lazy as a cuckoo
> as mazed (silly) as a sheep
> as old as St. Pauls
> as poor as a herring
> as proud as a louse

as quick as thought
as ragged as a ram
as silly as a waggon horse
as sour as a wig
as thirl (empty) as a greyhound
as weak as a wren
half as big as a bed bug

A few other miscellaneous expressions:

To use bad language is to 'curse flashes'.

Something going very fast can be described as going 'like a mowing machine'. This must reflect the wonder when the new agricultural machinery replaced the old hand methods.

'As near to fourpence as a groat' must now be obsolete.

Place names appear in some expressions as when 'Do you come from Purton' is shouted at anyone who leaves the door open. (Purton is a village in Wiltshire.) A saying equivalent to 'you can go to Hell' although milder in tone is 'You can go a ookey'. Is the last word a form of the name 'Wookey' of 'Wookey Hole' fame in Somerset, or is it the free infinitive of 'to uck', a sort of general-purpose verb with a sense of stirring something about and so the expression meant 'Get on with your own work'?

6 DIALECT AND SOCIETY

When asked what the function of a language is, the linguist usually replies that it 'mediates' the world for the speaker. This recognises the fact that it is more than just a means of communication, it is a way, for instance, of relieving strong feelings, like the swear-word we use when we hit our head on a low beam, and it gives, when necessary, a framework for our thoughts. It is no longer tenable that there are efficient (or logical) languages and inefficient ones, each being able to mediate precisely the environment in which it is used. So we must not look at dialect as a debased, slovenly or rustic form of English, but as an accurate reflection of the communities which used it. In this chapter we shall be looking through the words and expressions they used at the kind of life they led.

The world of the dialect speaker was a rural one, before the Industrial Revolution had impinged on it, before the rapid increase in population had taken place, when towns were small and intimately linked with the surrounding fields and when each community was to a large extent self-sufficient, growing or producing the majority of its needs. Life in this world was the lineal descendant of life in a medieval village, or of its Iron Age predecessor. It disappeared during the two wars of this century and the years between, but it was preparing itself for radical changes all through the nineteenth century with such events as the building of railways and the introduction of new agricultural machinery. People did not seem to realise the profundity of the changes that were taking place, and Hardy in one of his poems wrote of the old man harrowing the clods with his old horse as something that would never change 'though dynasties pass'. This world forms the background for many of our greatest novels, but it is only in our more self-conscious age that books of reminiscences have appeared, describing the last years of the old way of life. A notable example is Flora Thompson's trilogy *Lark Rise to Candleford*. Though this is set in south Oxfordshire, just outside our area, it presents a fascinating picture of rural life in the late nineteenth century.

The use of dialect declined with the disappearance of the society in which it was used, and the beginning of the process for each began in that rather vague historical event, the Industrial Revolution. Then horizons widened and the local forms of speech were no longer good enough. Formerly, the farmer who needed a new waggon ordered it from the local wheelwright and could talk to him about its *exes* (axles), its *hound* (the forecarriage) or its *thills* (the shafts); a miller who had to renew his millwheel or a clothier in a town who wanted a horse-wheel to drive his machinery, both had similar conversations. But when the latter ordered a new steam-engine from Messrs Boulton and Watt he had to use the standard terminology: 'piston', 'pressure gauge' and 'inlet-valve' do not admit of dialect forms. The effect of these mechanical improvements on the people in general was often one of wonderment, and one sees pictures of the crowd that turned out when, for example, water is laid on in a small town. Halliwell, in his Dictionary, gives examples of dialect writing, and one of those for Devonshire is a poem describing the reaction of a country couple when they 'cum up t'Exeter to zee the railway opened 1 May 1844'. Allowing for poetical exaggeration there is some truth in the astonishment these people felt, and, even taking into account the imperfections of written dialect, I think it is worth quoting in full.

'Lor Johnny! lor Johnny! now whativver es that,
    A urning[1] along like a hoss upon wheels?
'Tis as bright as yer buttons, and black as yer hat,
    And jist listen, Johnny, and yer how 'a squeals!'

'Dash my buttons, Moll—I'll be darned if I know;
    Us was vools to come yerr and to urn into danger,
Let's be off—'a spits vire! lor, do let us go—
    And 'a holds up his head like a gooze at a stranger!'

'I be a bit vrighten'd—but let us bide yerr;
    And hark how 'a puffs, and caughs, and 'a blows,
He edden unlike the old cart-hoss last yer—
    Broken-winded,—and yet only zee how 'a goes!

'"A urns upon ladders, with they things like wheels,
    Or hurdles, or palings, put down on the ground;
But why do they let 'un stray out of the veels?
    'Tis a wonder they don't clap 'un into the pound."'

'"A can't be alive, Jan—I don't think 'a can."'
    'I bain't zure o' that, Moll, for jist look'ee how
'A breathes like a hoss, or znivell'd old man:—
    And hark how he's bust out a caughing, good now.

---

[1] urn = run.

Wessex Dialect

' "A never could dra' all they waggins, d'ee zee,
  If 'a lived upon vatches, or turmets, or hay;
Why, they waggins be vill'd up with people—they be;
  And do 'ee but look how they'm larfin away!

'And look to they children a urning about,
  Wi' their mouths vull of gingerbread, there by the zhows;
And zee to the scores of vine ladies turn'd out;
  And gentlemen, all in their best Zunday clothes.

'And look to this houze made o' canvas zo zmart;
  And the dinner zet out with such bussle and fuss;—
But us brought a squab pie, you know, in the cart,
  And a keg of good zider—zo that's nort to us.

'I tell 'ee what 'tis, Moll—this here is my mind,
  The world's gone quite maze, as zure as you'm born;
'Tis as true as I'm living—and that they will vind,
  With their hosses on wheels that don't live upon corn.

'I wouldn't go homeward b'mbye to the varm
  Behind such a critter, when all's zed and dun,
We've a travell'd score miles, but we never got harm,
  Vor there's nort like a market cart under the zun.'

Before we set out on our picture of life of the dialect speakers, a word of warning must be given. In general words refer to areas of meaning, which have been specialised in different ways in the various parts of the south-west. For example, *maund* is a basket, but some users state categorically that it means a feeding-basket for horses only, while others use it for a clothes-basket and in some areas it is the basket used to carry food to the fields for the workmen. In the following account some readers may find words used in, what is according to them, the 'wrong' sense, but if so I can assure them that the use I make of the word is well attested in one part of our area. In the course of my investigations I have been surprised over and over again to find that other people did not conform to the usage of a word or phrase that I had been accustomed to since I was a child, but I think we must follow the principle of modern linguistics, and take a very broad view and accept as correct what the native speaker says whether it coincides with our personal idea of what is right or not.

The West Country is one of the main milk-producers of England, the wetter conditions suiting the growth of grass in the lowlands. However, there are large stretches of drier downland, and it is said that the expression 'the difference between chalk and cheese' originated in Wiltshire and refers to the high downs compared with the milk-producing valleys. Let us begin by looking at dairying. The cows can be *dummocks* or *hummocks* and they are housed in a *pine*, a *shippon*, a (lean-to) *skeeling* or a *boosing*, which may have a *cratch* in it to hold their hay. They were looked after by a *fogger*, originally a groom whose job was also to tend the cattle, but now still occasionally used in Hampshire as a cowman. Lush grass is produced in *floating meadows*, irrigated by a system of *carriages* and *drawns*, but fodder for the winter must be provided at haymaking. The grass is cut and raked into lines, called *rollers, wallows, hatches* or, in Cornwall *drams*. It is finally made into cocks or *pooks*, to await loading on to a cart with a *two-grained prong*, that is a two-tined fork, to be taken to the rick or *mow*. The end of the harvest is often marked by a feast, but the villagers who turned out in the last century to help with the busy times of haymaking could expect a *pookers' tea*. Milk can be made into cheese, and that needs rennet or *ernet* (a metathesised form), or calves trins or *calf poke*—the calf's stomach, which is a source of rennet. Cream or *ream* is skimmed off pans with a reamer and churned into butter.

To a townsman, the animals on a farm fall into simple categories such as pigs, sheep or cows, but the farmer needs to differentiate between their age and their breeding capacity. A *chilver*, although the word is related to 'calf' is a ewe lamb, and a *chilver-hog* the same up to the age of two years. Then comes a complicated system of *two-tooths* and *four-tooths* with many dialectal variants. A young sow is called a *hilt*.

It was pleasant on a recent visit to Dorsetshire to see hurdles still in use giving shelter that no chain-link fence could give. When they were used for folding sheep they were fixed to a stake driven into the ground called a *fossel* or *vossel*, forms of *foldsail,* a *sail* being the upright bar in a hurdle itself. Hurdles could stand up to sheep, but if cattle had to be penned, or if a more permanent partition was needed, a *flake* was used. This was a frame with ash or willow spars, resembling a light gate. Hedges could not be neglected, but had to be laid or plashed or *spleeshed*. This consisted of partly cutting through some of the upright growths, bending them over and weaving them in and out of stakes set in the ground and holding them in place with *ethers* or *edders*, made of pliant hazel rods.

Wessex Dialect

Pigs have long played a large part in the economy of the south-west and still do. A typical product of the area is the lardy cake made, as the name implies, with lard and usually known as *fat cakes*. Pigs are kept in the *pig-lewze* or the *pig's crow* in Cornwall, but in the open they *howk up* or *uck up* roots with their snouts. Until well after the war I was often sent to the butcher's to buy a pound of pig's liver off *the henge*. This was the windpipe to which was attached the liver, the lights and the heart. I presume the word is associated with 'to hang' because the windpipe was hung by a hook to a bar, and this might link it with the 'Hanging Stones' of Stonehenge.

In the days of self-sufficiency, corn was grown in every village. The first necessity was to ensure the fertility of the land. Dung was taken to the fields in a *dung-putt* (dung cart) and *spurled* (spread) with an *evil* (a dung fork). Another method was Devonshiring, so called because it originated in that county, but the word is usually written *denshering* and pronounced as indicated by that spelling. This process consisted or paring off the top layer of turf and burning it, leaving the ash to fertilise the ground. In spite of its west-country origin it is usually called in our area *burnbake*, the second part, although having an apparent a logical connection with the first, is none-the-less from the verb 'beak' to break up. In the days before compost heaps in gardens were common, in the autumn when the potatoes were being dug, all the haulms were put on a huge bonfire that lasted several days and left a large pile of ash that we called *burny-bake*.

The lands were ploughed, perhaps with a *sole, sully* or *zully*, made of wood. The first furrow *veered* out of the land, that is marked it out with a furrow, *veer* being probably the same word as furrow that has lost its ending like other similar words. Ploughing was done in *rudges* (ridges) and the last strip left was the *ent*, which was *hinted* or halved, one half being turned one way and one half the other. The arch enemy of the farmer in his fields of grain was birds. Two methods of control were used, how successfully I do not know. A scarecrow—that is a *gallicrow* or a *gallibagger* (from *gally*, to frighten), a *dudman* (dressed in rags), a *bugalo*, a *bugabo* or in Cornwall, a *bucca*—stood in the fields. Or a boy could be employed, armed with a pair of *clackers* (clappers) to make a noise.

> *I up bi' me clackers,*
> *And hit the bird back'ards*

was, no doubt, wishful thinking. The latter was called *bird-keeping*, but sometimes, and more realistically, *bird-starving*.

Reaping was done many years ago with a *shekel*, a short-bladed sickle with a serrated ege. The corn was held in the crook of the arm and the shekel drawn towards the reaper with a saw-like motion. It could be sharpened with a *grind-stone apple*, a crab-apple through which the blade was drawn, the acid biting into the steel. It was superseded by the *reap-hook*, the ordinary sickle of today, with the blade extending well beyond the line of the handle and used with a crooked stick, and also, of course, by the scythe.

The grain was tied up in sheaves which were stood up to dry in *hiles* (stooks or shocks), in an operation known as *hiling, goating, stitching* or *stocking*. At the appropriate time, the hiles were carted and built into ricks or *mows* ('stacks' is not used in the south-west), to await threshing. Each rick had to be thatched. *Elms* or *yealms*, that is bundles of straw, were prepared and fixed to the rick with hazel spars or *spicks*, and straw rope, made locally with a *wimble*.

A *mow* was often a rick, but in some parts it was the part of a barn, a large bay at either end, where the corn was kept under cover. The space in between the *mows* was the *midstay*, or *midstead*. This was the threshing-floor, and big doors on either side gave the necessary current of air for winnowing. The threshing itself was done with a flail or *dreshel* or *threshol*, that is two pieces of wood with an eelskin universal joint, hence often known as a *pair of dreshels*, the handle being longer than the beater, which accounts for its other name, a *stick and a half*. The threshed grain had to be *wimmed* (winnowed) by being thrown up in a current of air so that the heavier grain was separated from the lighter *cavings* (chaff). Then it was stored in a *tallet*, usually a loft over a stable or similar building, but sometimes the word was used to refer to a special granary that stood on staddle stones. Corn sold by volume, in bushels, and the bushel-measure was filled and the grain levelled off with a *strickle* or *stritch*. Great care was taken to see that the grain did not settle in the measure more than could be helped or the buyer would get more than necessary, so the strickle had to be used with great care. If one of the men happened to touch the measure with his shovel it was emptied and filling started all over again.

One of the most useful draught animals was the donkey, known as a *mokus, nessock* or *nirrup*. In the farmyard—the *barken* perhaps—stood the *linhay* (cartshed).

The air was filled with the calls of the animals. Horses would *wicker, nutter, bray* or even *whistle*, bulls and cows would *belve* or *bleat* and sheep would *bleak*.

Wessex Dialect

The long days spent in the fields, especially at harvest time, are in evidence in the names of the various snacks, the *crib* or *crust*, the *bait* or *tommy* that the farm worker took with him. *Crib, crust, bait* and *tommy* all mean 'food'. In England we are never quite certain about our meals, whether we have 'dinner' in the middle of the day or the evening. In the country *lunch* is had at mid-morning, what is known in R.S. as 'elevenses'. The farm worker was out early, and by his mid-morning, i.e. about nine o'clock, he was ready for his *dewbit*. This lasted until well past midday, although the second meal he had was *nammit*, a corruption of 'noon-meat'. In some areas the order of snacks was reversed, *nammit* being eaten before *dewbit*. No doubt both meals consisted of a *hunch* of bread (a form of 'hunk), with cheese. For drink, he carried cider or beer in a *plough bottle* or *costeril*—originally a leather bottle, but later replaced by an earthenware cruse or a small wooden barrel, which was still called a *plough bottle*. If there had been an inn nearby, which offered, as even those in central London do today, a 'ploughman's lunch', he may well have asked 'What sort of *tackle* (food) d'ee call this?' When the day's work was done, being a west-country man, he cried *whey*, not 'whoa', to his horses, and set off for home.

Home was a cottage, thatched probably, with deep *oaves* (eaves). The main room was the kitchen where the cooking was done, the children played and the family sat in the evening. They may have called the bedroom the *chamber*. The source of water was a well or a *plump* (pump). One important part of the house was separated from the rest; this was the earth-closet—the *dunnekin*, the *duddekin* or the *dyke*. Even when piped water was brought to the towns and the larger villages, the *dunnekin* remained at the bottom of the garden for many years. Since so much effort had to be made to keep out the rain and the damp—which made the door *plim* (swell), it was foolish to bring water inside deliberately. In the house where I was born there was no water laid on, there was a W.C. at the bottom of the garden and a standpipe served eight houses. Even standpipes were not always welcome. One countryman argued that he would much rather be occupied drawing up water from a well than stand, twiddling his thumbs, while his bucket filled from a tap.

The central point of the kitchen was the fireplace, the source of all heat in the house, of all hot water and where the cooking was done. In my home we had constant hot water, not that we had an imersion heater or central heating, but a large iron kettle or *polly* stood over the fire. The fire had to lit every morning with the aid of *faggotwood* or *puffs*, and the ashes *ruddered* (sieved or riddled) to save any cinders big enough to be put on again. From time to time it had to be replenished (to *beet* the fire was how it used to be said), when one would put on coal and *chumps* or *plocks* (logs). These last could often be had for nothing or at least at a very low price, and a saying of my childhood was:

> He that do love his home
> Do bring a stick or a stone.

By the side of or over the fire was the oven. Some cottages had bread ovens, which were heated by putting inside and burning *bavins* (faggots of wood), the ash and charcoal being swept out with a *mawkin* before the bread was put in. There was no thermometer on the oven door, but to tell whether the temperature was right, a *gauge brick* was put in which showed by its change of colour if the heat was great enough. Meanwhile, the fire was kept up, the *blankers* flew about to the delight of the children, and the smoke *tundled* out of the *tun* (chimney). Cooking over an open fire had its hazards, as is recognised by the parody of 'While shepherds watched' we used to sing as children:

> 'While shepherds watched their pot by night,
> A boiling turnip tops,
> A lump of soot came down the tun
> And spoilt the blooming lot.'

On the *clavy* or *clavy tack* (mantlepiece), which may well have been over six feet from the ground, stood vases full of oddments, and china dogs, and in the middle was a clock.

Washing-up was done in the *trough*—the pronunciation trow [troʊ] is universal in the south-west—and the water was thrown down the *sink* (drain). The *shoot* or *launder* (the down-pipe from the guttering or the guttering itself) also ran into the *sink* if there was no water-butt. In the kitchen various receptacles were used for storage and preparation—*hutches, stugs, yusens* or *bussas*, and when, for instance, a stove required filling, the housewife sought her *tunigar* or *tundish* (funnel) to help her. When clothes had been washed they were carried out in a *clothes flask* and hung on a line strung between two *lineposts*.

When the man of the house came in he was, no doubt, *main lear* (very hungry), and attention must be given to food. Much of it would have been home-produced, including the *chetties* (the potatoes, merely a variant of that word, developed by way of 'taters), the *gibbles* or *scalions* (spring onions) as well as other vegetables. Many cottagers kept a pig which, when it was at last killed, provided a feast:

> *Ower fiather's gwain ta kill tha pig*
> *When he comes wom tonight,*
> *An lore tha thoughts on it da vill*
> *I up we mad delight.*

wrote Edward Slow, the Wiltshire poet, in 'The Girt Vat Pig',

> *Ah 'tis a appy time a twoam*
> *Wen we da kill a pig,*
> *Var zich nice veasten I da av,*
> *Wich meaks I grow za big.*

He goes on to list the products, the 'pettitoes' (trotters), 'girt black puddens vine', 'vagots', 'chidlins', 'pig's vry' and 'griskin'. Then the sides go into a *zilt*, to be salted so that they will not eventually become *rasty, rafty* or *rutchy* (rancid). The faggots are wrapped in the fat from around the pig's kidneys, the *apron, flare* or *fleck,* although we always called it *caul fat* (we often pronounced it as 'coal fat', but, then, if it was wrong to say 'knaw' and right to say 'know', why should we not talk grand even in the humble matter of faggots?). This fat was suitable for rendering into lard, and then little bits of meat that were left, the scraps or *scratchings* or *graves*, were considered a real delicacy. Caul fat is becoming hard to get these days, but *chitlins*, or rather chitterlings, can be bought pre-packed, so that the usual request 'all knotling and no bag please' is now useless. *Knotling*, a word also used for chitterlings, was the intestine and the less prized *bag* were the large flat pieces of udder. At Christmas, we always had a *vorspur* (forespur, the hock of pork).

After the main course, a good *figgy pudden* or *figgety duff* was welcome (*figs* are raisins). Most people enjoyed a cup of tea, as long as it had not been left too long in the pot, when it would be *sammed* (stewed), and the *gruts, grouts* or, in Cornwall the *groushans*, would have to be thrown down the *sink*.

As I have said, most of the food would be home-produced and many people had an allotment, the usual size of which was ten *lug* (rods, poles or perches—just over 300 square yards). Cottage gardens were gay with flowers, such as *dogsmouths* (antirrhinums), *bleeding hearts* (red wallflowers), *hen and chicken* (London pride) and *golden chain* (laburnum). These and other flowers could be made into *tutties* (posies, although the word was also used for the flower itself) or *peepshows* —flowers were placed between a piece of cardboard and a piece of glass, and the edges bound with tape. But the main function of a garden was the production of food, and many of our dialect speakers would have looked with amazement at those of today's gardens which are devoted entirely to flowers. Nor did the cottage garden observe the same sharp distinction between flowers and vegetables, both flourishing side-by-side in the same plot. The gardener attacked his plot with a *tomahawk* or *tommy hacker* (not the Indian weapon, but a hoe with a long, thin blade, rather like an adze, or in some parts, a fork the tines of which are bent at 90° to the handle), useful for breaking up the ground before earthing-up potatoes, especially if the earth was *clit* (hardened on the top, as after rain). The tools my father used were not the smart tools of today, but were often handed down from father to son, or home-made. A useful turf-cutter could be made by cutting an old panel saw about six inches below the handle (you had to get down on your knees to use it) and the broken handle of a spade could be turned into a *pogger* (dibber), used to *pog* holes for plants—that is brassicas. A *prong* (fork) was essential for many tasks, including the removal of *rumblers*, that is potatoes that have accidently grown from those left in the ground the previous season. Another source of free food was in the harvest fields, after the corn had been carted, when the villagers were allowed to go *leasing* (gleaning). Food from the wild included mushrooms, the dialect forms *musheroons* or *mushers* showing that the word is derived from the French word 'mousseron'.

Dialect reflects a society where farming was the occupation of the majority, but there were, of course, other trades. One of the most important figures in the village was the *millard* (miller), often a rather aloof character isolated in his mill, which often stood away from the village, amid his vibrating machinery, with mysterious names like the *wallower* or the *damsel*. One of his jobs was to turn over the heavy top-stone of his pair of mill stones, in order to recut the grooves necessary to grind the corn. For this he used a *mill-peck*, a hammer-like instrument, and as a preliminary, in order to get a perfectly flat surface, he used a long straight-edge, the mill-staff, rubbed with *ruddle, reddle, redding* or *erding*, the red dye that was used to mark sheep, and which Digory Venn sold in Hardy's *Return of the Native*. The miller took in a quantity of corn and, of necessity, returned a smaller amount of flour. He was always suspected of keeping some of it back for his own use and so giving short measure, and was commonly mistrusted. Thus children in Devonshire used to sing:

Millardy, millardy, dowsty poll
How many pecks hev you a-stole?

'Dowsty poll' (poll means head), refers to the fact that the miller was usually covered in a fine white film of flour.

Another skilled craftsman was the wheelwright, who made waggons, carts or *putts*. A *put* or *pot* was a two-wheeled tipping cart used for taking manure to the fields. Originally it was carried in two pots slung across a horse's back and when wheels came into use the name was transferred. These locally-made vehicles had a vocabulary all their own—the *hound* (the forepart to which the shafts were connected, the wheels turning to guide the cart), the *dripples* or *thripples* (the sides or sometimes the ladders that are fixed on to the ends when a load of hay has to be carried), the *sharps* (shafts) and many other words, formerly commonplace, but now almost forgotten. The saddler or harness-maker had his special terms, too, words such as *wanty* or *ganty*, the breeching or *berching* and the names of the various parts of the harness for the *diller* (a shaft-horse) or the trace-horse.

Dialect names of clothing reflect the outdoor life most men led. There are several words for gaiters, *bams, strads* and *stogs*. *Yorks* were straps tied around the trousers, just below the knee, to stop them trailing in the mud.

When we move to the larger villages and the small towns, where rural industry was centred, we find less evidence of the life in dialect. Along the Wiltshire/Somersetshire border are found *blind houses*, a local name for a one- or two-celled lock-up. A more widespread word is *drung*—a passageway between buildings. Dialect research has always concentrated on agriculture and daily life and has comparatively neglected other spheres of man's activities. The probable fields where investigation may very well prove fruitful are the age-old industries, fishing, mining and cloth-making. This last was fairly widespread in Wiltshire, Somersetshire and Gloucestershire until the end of the last century, and even today there are two centres where cloth is still woven, west Wiltshire and Gloucestershire. Some of the terms used were definitely peculiar to the south-west. One that reminds us of the less mechanised days is *seg* or *sig*. This is urine used in the scouring process, and a familiar sight was the *seg cart* which went the rounds collecting urine from workhouses, public houses and from private households. Although this method was superseded by an invention of 1833, the seg cart survived until the last years of the nineteenth century. The folk-memory lasted even longer, for when I was a child before the second World War, if I happened to put my mouth near any piece of woollen cloth I was told in no uncertain terms how unhygienic it was. Another now superseded process was the raising of the nap by the use of teasels. The ordinary teasels of the fields were not used, but special, stiffer cultivated ones. (About half an acre of these teasels are still grown in the Langport area of Somersetshire.) Teasels were divided by size into *kings* and *middles* (or *thousands*). Thirty king teasels made a *gleen*, 30 gleens made a *stave* and 30 staves a *pack*. For middles the number in each case was 40.

When cloth is woven the stationary threads on the loom are usually known as the warp, and the shuttle, passing between the alternate threads of the warp in a gap called the shed, produces the weft. In the west-country the warp is known as the *chain* and the weft as the *shoot*. Another and older word for the weft is the *abb*. The shed, the opening through which the shuttle passes, is produced by a number of harnesses, horizontal bars that can be raised and lowered, thus raising and lowering the threads of the warp. To do this each thread is connected to the harness by a wire, called in the west country a *heddle* (in the North they are known as *healds*). The thread of the weft is wound on a bobbin in the shuttle and this bobbin is a *quill*. *Quill winding* is one of the processes of the cloth industry.

A few other terms are peculiar to the west-country cloth mills; the *list* is the selvedge of the cloth, *spile* is the vegetable matter found in wool and *braying* is scouring cloth after it has been woven.

Coal-mining and fishing too have their specialised vocabularies although, because of the movement of men between one mining area and another and one part of the coast and another, terms are not confined to one particular area, and so we are moving into the area of occupational instead of regional dialects. In the Somerset coalfield, a mine is a *gruff*, but this is a form of *grove*, used in the midland coalfields. In Cornwall fishing boats are called *toshers*, a name also found in East-Anglia. Some mining terms are also found in agricultural contexts, an example being *guss*, a saddle-girth, but used in the Somerset coalfield in the phrase *guss and crook*. This was a strap similar to a girth, but fastened round the waist of the unfortunate boy whose job it was to haul the 'tram' loaded with coal back to the foot of the shaft. To the front of the *guss* was attached a chain with a hook on the end, and the chain passed between the boy's legs (he had to stoop most of the time) and was hooked on to the tram.

Cornish tin-mining supplies more local words. Lately we have heard on the news of the closure of the Wheal Grace mine. *Wheal* is commonly found in the names of mines. A *bal* is a working and *bal-maidens* women who worked at ground-level. *Stoping* is removing ore from the lode and then it is 'brought to grass'. *Tut-work* is piece-work.

Villagers and townspeople took a great interest in the affairs of their neighbours. Communities thought it fitting to give expression to their disapproval of unsatisfactory aspects of marriages, such as wife-beating, henpecking or even beating of the husband or infidelity. They did this with a *skimmety ride* or *skimmington*, also called *rough music* or a *hooset*. This demonstration could have various forms and different elements. One of these elements was rough music, 'a discordant din of sticks, pans and a heterogeneous collection of instruments [such as] frying pans, bulls' horns, marrow bones and cleavers' (Halliwell). With this went the burning of effigies of the offenders and a procession, sometimes on horseback, sometimes with a symbolic horse's head. Halliwell gives a description of one such 'in ridicule of a man beaten by a woman. It consists of a man riding behind a woman with his face to the horse's tail, holding a distaff in his hand, at which he seems to work, the woman all the while beating him with a ladle. A smock displayed is carried before them as an emblematical standard denoting female superiority'. It is said that the demonstration took place on three nights, followed by an interval of three nights, another three performances, another interval of three nights and finally the 'serenade' presented for a further three nights. What an effort of organisation must have been required! Those I know of were simpler affairs. In fact, although such events have taken place in Holland in the last ten years, the last I have heard of in the south-west occured during the First World War. An eye-witness sent me this account: 'I saw the incident you mentioned. She lived in — Street and worked at — . She had stayed with a soldier in — for the weekend. When she went to work after dinner on Monday the workers were waiting for her. They tied a rope round her waist and dropped her in the river, then they put her on a truck and wheeled her through the town. I thought they called it a ducking, but my son said it was a skimmety. I know of two other skimmeties. They made a big bonfire outside the homes of the people and my mother has told me that hundreds of people would gather around with big sticks and poke it up. My brother took part in one—he was coming home from choir practice'.

A skimmety is described in Hardy's novel *The Mayor of Casterbridge.*

And so the years came and went and the seasons followed each other. The winter was marked by *daggers, daglets* or *conkerbells* (icicles), and the snow *pitched* (settled—the word is also used for a method of paving) before it *unthawed.* Summer may have brought a period of *dryth* (drought). April saw its characteristic showers, or if they were shorter and sharper than usual perhaps they were *scuds.* Harvest and haymaking were important events in the prosperity of the countryside. I remember coming home from school in June and hearing an unfamiliar clanking. The heart quickened at the thought that it might be a steamroller, but once a year it was the noise made by the old-fashioned mowing machine, drawn by a plodding old carthorse, yet often used as a simile for speed—*to go like a mowing machine.* I have found in the south-west the retention, as in East-Anglia, of Old Lady Day, or Old Michaelmas Day, that is 13 days later than they are at present, as would have been the case if the calendar had not been reformed in 1752; but Old Christmas Day is still recognised in some parts on 6 January. Christmas Eve is known as *Ashen Faggot Night* in some areas of Somersetshire. Saints' days were not allowed to pass unnoticed and the appropriate buttonhole was worn, even shamrock for such an alien saint as Patrick. 29 May is Oak Apple Day, commemorating King Charles II who hid in an oak tree at Boscobel. In the south-west it is called *Shitsack* or *Shickshack* Day (*shitsack* = oak apple) and children wore a sprig of young oak leaves in the morning and *Even Ash*, a twig of ash with an even number of leaflets, in the afternoon. I doubt whether these customs are observed any more, but there is always the village festival, whether it is the flower show, the feast, the fête, the *revel* or the *randy* held on a particular day in the year. We might also mention the vigorous tradition of the town or village carnival in the south-west . The picturesque survival, in Hungerford, Berkshire, of commers' rights and associated ceremonies with *tutti-men* who have poles wreathed with flowers (tutty = flower) is an old custom still going strong. Lowesly, in his *Berkshire Words* written in 1888, mentions two other old customs, the *Curvew Bell* which could still be heard in Blewberry, and the *Low Bell*, rung in the Vale of Berkshire by the herdsman who was appointed to take charge of cattle to be turned out on the Downs for grazing during the day. The bell announced that the cattle were to be delivered to him.

One yearly event that fortunately no longer takes place is *Cock Squoiling* on Shrove Tuesday. A *squailer* or *squoil* was a throwing stick. To make one a piece of ash about 15 in. long was held in a tea-cup while molten lead was poured round it. When the lead cooled, it left a heavy, conical knob round the end of the stick. It was used by boys for throwing at small game—rabbits, hares or squirrels—and birds, and for knocking apples off trees. In the right hands it could be an accurate and fearsome weapon. Ackerman, writing in 1842, talks of the 'barbarous custom of throwing at cocks, formerly a custom at Shrovetide'. He goes on, 'This unmanly pastime is, I fear, not entirely abolished in some part of England. I have seen poor, unfledged nestlings of small birds stuck upon a post and thrown at by countrymen'. The squailer was associated with Marlborough, especially with Marlborough College, which is perhaps why Goddard and Dartnell in *A Glossary of Wiltshire Words* quote, under *skug* (a squirrel), 'I say, there's a skug. Let's have a cockshot at him with your squailer' in a mixture of Public School English and dialect.

Children were, of course, an important part of the dialect-speaking world. They had their own dialect words, such as *ahmoos* (cows), or *coupies* (chickens) which lay *coupy eggs*. *Puddies* (hands) got hurt or, more frequently, needed to be washed. The word contrasted with *pakes*, which could be used for the hands of a grown-up. Children's games included *dibs*, played with knucklebones, and *tippet*, a party game, known more generally as 'Up Jenkins', in which one team of three tries to guess the position of an object such as a button or a threepenny-bit held in the tightly closed fists of the opposing team. Children's rhymes and superstitions abound. One was used by girls to ascertain the occupation of their future husbands. After the first Sunday in May—Cowslip Sunday—they picked cowslips and made them into a ball with soft wool. The balls were tossed in the flat of the hand, while the following was said:

> *Tisty-Tosty, tell me true,*
> *Who shall I be married to?*
> *Tinker, tailor, soldier, sailor, etc.*

The point at which the ball was dropped gave the answer to the question. The ladybird brought good luck, and the rhyme ran:

> *God a'mighty's colly cow[1]*
> *Fly up to heaven,*
> *Carry up ten pound*
> *And bring down eleven.*
>
> [1]colly cow = lady bird

One remedy still known among children is the dock leaf that will soothe
nettle stings. Hampshire boys 'and girls used to sing:

> *Out 'ettle[1], in dock,*
> *Dock shall ha' a new smock,*
> *'Ettle shan't ha' varun.*
>
> [1]'Ettle = nettle.

Children's rhymes are sometimes riddles. 'Humpty-Dumpty' is an example known to everyone (you had to guess what all the King's horses and
all the King's men could not put together, the answer being, of course, an
egg). Here is a similar rhyme in dialect, also from Hampshire:

> *Sieve upon herder[1],*
> *One upon the other,*
> *Noles[2] upon both sides,*
> *Not all the way through,*
> *What may it be?*
> *Say if you know.*

[1]herder = a metatheoised form of the dialect word *rudder*, which means a sieve, and is a
form of the R.S. 'riddle'.
[2]noles = holes.

The answer is a HONEYCOMB.

Toys do not figure largely in dialect, only perhaps marbles, which were
classified into common *clays*, the more prized *stoners* (the other spelling
that one meets, 'stwoners', gives a better idea of the usual pronunciation),
and the best of all, the *alleys* (short for 'alabaster'). If the latter had a
fleck of red, they were known as *blood alleys*. One children's pastime was
to *dap* (bounce) a ball as many times as possible, and a button spinning
round on a piece of wool provided much entertainment. The latter were
known as a *fizzgig* or a *whirligig*.

The world of Nature is well represented in dialect, with local names for
many flowers and other plants, as well as insects and animals.
Goosegrass has tiny hooks on its leaves and fruits, which cause them to
cling to the clothing, and this fact accounts for the name *sweethearts*.
Sticky Buttons is another and similar name for the plant. The blue Germander Speedwell is called *birdseye*, the cowslip becomes the more
earthy *cowslop* or *cowflop*. The bane of gardeners, bindweed or con-
vulvulus, has many local names, as noted in a previous chapter; those
which are variants of *willowind* or *withywind* remind us of the word

withy, in R.S. osiers for basket-making, but in the south-west, the common name for a willow tree. *Stroil* (couch grass) is another persistent weed. Amongst animals, a *skug* is a squirrel, a *fairy* or *fitch* a polecat and a *sherry* or *harvest row* a shrew mouse. 'As fat as a want' (a mole) is a common simile. In the nothern part of our area, the form *'oont* is more usual. One word for a bat, *flittermouse*, recalls the German fledermaus but they are also known as by such words as *rear mouse* or *rye mouse*, while in Cornwall *ekkymowl* is used. In ponds and streams we can find *tomtoddies* or *poheads* (tadpoles) and *evets* (newts), as well as *bannistickles* (sticklebacks). Insects are represented in dialect by *emmets* (ants), known in Cornwall as *muryans*, and by the many names for the woodlouse—*bakers, croogers, gladdigoasters* and the name by which I knew them, *gramfers*.

It often seems that this self-sufficient, unhurried life contrasts attractively with our own noisy, artificial environment, but, for me, our present society has one advantage which outweighs any other inconvenience and that is the standard of medical care. For the dialect speaker pain, infant mortality and early death were very much part of his experience, as any graveyard will show.

> *Pain was my portion,*
> *And physic was my food;*
> *Groans were my devotion,*
> *But drugs did me no good.*

reads a west-country epitaph. 'Never so well after the knife' reflects the common opinion of a surgical operation. Diphtheria and Scarlet Fever were widespread and *Whitemouth* (Thrush) a killer. This last is, perhaps, due to lack of hygiene, when sterilising agents were not so easily obtainable, and a number of words describe slight skin infections. Boils are *ampers, apses* or *pinswells* (pronounced 'pinsles'), styes on the eye *wisps* or *quailaways* and a pimply person was said to be *ampery*. A *nimpingang* (whitlow) was thought to be caused by milking. Lung infections were rife, including Tuberculosis, and a large number of words describe coughing—*tizzicking* (perhaps connected with the word 'phthisis'), *hackling, hasking, hicketing*—or being hoarse—*hoozed* or *oozling*. Life and work outdoors left their marks—*bladders* (blisters), *childags* or *springdags* (chilblains), and the fact that the hands were often *spreethed* or *sprayed*. This last is a soreness of the back of the hand caused by wind and cold and the dialect speaker feels that the usual equivalent in R.S. is a not very exact replacement for a useful word. Strange diseases like *megrims* or *colliwobbles* (migraine or diarrhoea) beset the days of the country dweller, as well as a *niddy-noddy* or *St Viper's Dance* (any illness involving the 'shakes').

To combat these conditions recourse could be had to certain home-made remedies such as *blackberry vinegar* against colds (the bitter taste was worse than any cold, but I suppose it contained vitamin C). Houseleek provided a lotion for eye-infections, and fumitory or *fevertory* could be distilled to make a cosmetic for removing freckles:

> *If you wish to be pure and holy,*
> *Wash your face with fevertory.*

In case of bed-wetting (or worse), the dandelion was considered to be of help, hence its dialect names of *pissabed* or *shitabed* (cf. French pissenlit).

The body had its special words, the throat being the *kecker* (from the dialect verb *keck*, to retch), or the *quilter* (from the dialect verb *quilt*, to swallow). In Devonshire it was the *oozle* and in Cornwall the *klunker* (from the Cornish verb *klunk*, a word borrowed from the old Cornish language). Hands are *pakes* (or *puddies* when speaking to children) ears are *busses* or *wickers*, and the *niddick* is the neck. Defects are well represented, too, with *napkneed* (knockneed), *hen-toed* (pigeon-toed) and the many expressions for 'left-handed'—*cunnyhanded, keckhanded* and *marlborough-handed*, to quote but a few.

This, then, was the world of the dialect speaker, mainly rural in background, with its market towns, its 'vernacular' industry and its local craftsmen, but where agriculture was the predominant concern. Dialect reflects the everyday life of these people, their homes, their gardens, their food, their health, their children and their pastimes. It was a world of few changes where the pace of life was slow and horizons were limited. One feels that dialect was much more suitable for discussing the affairs of the neighbours than for moral arguments or political discourse. Vast changes have been wrought in this life by the two wars and the social changes of this century. Has the old life disappeared, or does it still linger on in the villages and in the lives of old people? Have we passed through a watershed, after which things will never be even remotely recognisable; or when further years have elapsed, shall we discern a continuity of life pattern or even of speech patterns between the dialect-speaking world and the society which has replaced it?

A GLOSSARY OF DIALECT WORDS

A list of words is what most people look for in a book on dialect and they do, indeed, form the most notable and most memorable feature of regional speech. However, I pointed out in chapter 5 the difficulties of studying dialect vocabulary. To ransack tne various glossaries or the English Dialect Dictionary would be to produce a list that would be several times longer than this book. To select words is to run the risk of pleasing nobody. In this glossary, I have been guided by the following considerations: 1) I have tried to include words still, or recently, in use, either from my own experience or from evidence given in source books; 2) words that illustrate points made in the earlier chapters of the book have also been given a place; 3) a few words have been listed because of their intrinsic interest; and 4), I have included a small number of words from various sources which I have not been able to find in any other work of reference, in the hope that someone else will recognise them and that they will be eventually added to our dialect vocabularies. In some cases I have suggested an area where a word is in use. This is very tentative, especially when it has to be done in the context of counties, the only possible framework. For a more accurate distribution, a map is needed and such a one for the word *want* (mole) is to be found on p. 45.

ABB (n.) in a loom, the weft, the thread carried by the shuttle.

ABEAR (vb.) to bear, used only with 'cannot', e.g. *I can't abear the sight on 'un*. Probably a combination of *bear* and *abide*.

AFEARD, AVEARD (adj.) afraid. The usual form in the south-west.

AFORE (prep. and adv.) before.

AGG. (vb.) to cut clumsily. A form of *hack*.

AGLONS (n. pl.) haws, the berries of the hawthorn. There are other, similar forms of this word.

AHMOO (n.) a cow, a children's word.

AIRY MOUSE (n.) a bat (mammal). See also *Rear Mouse*.

ALLEMANG (adj.) mixed up, as 'when two flocks of sheep are driven together accidentally' (Goddard and Dartnell). Used now, I believe, in square dancing.

ALL-A-HOH (adj.) lop-sided, awry or even upset.

ALLEY (n.) a marble. This is a short form of *alabaster*. Children's marbles are divided into *stoners, clays* or *alleys*. If the latter has a fleck of red, it is a 'Blood Alley'.

AMPER (n.) a tumour, boil or blister.

AMPERY (adj.) unhealthy looking, pimply.

ANEWST (adv.) nearly.

ANUNT (prep.) opposite or beside.

ANYWHEN (adv.) any time. Formed on the same principle as R.S. 'anywhere', but not adopted by the standard language. See *Somewhen*.

APPLE BEE (n.) a wasp. A Devonshire word.

APPLE DRANE, APPLE DRONE (n.) a wasp. Devonshire and Cornwall.

APRON (n.) the internal fat of a pig, used for wrapping faggots. Also known as *Flare, Flay, Flead* and *Caul Fat*.

APS (n.) an aspen. This is a metathesised form, although it may be the older of the two.

APS (n.) a boil.

ARG (vb.) to argue. The word has lost its ending, like 'carry' (*car* in dialect) or 'empty' (*empt*). The old pronunciation was 'arguy' ('argy-bargy' is a reduplicated form), and the -y was dropped by analogy with the ending of the free infinitive (see Chap. 4, Grammar).

ARRISH (n.) stubble, a stubble field. Also found as *Errish* or *Eddish*.

ARSE SMART (n.) Redleg, *Polygonum Persicaria L.* or Water-Pepper, *Polygonum Hydropiper L.* But sometimes bindweed. Also found as YES SMART. Halliwell (1848) quotes from an older publication: 'If a handful of Arsmart be put on a tired horse's back it will make him travaille fresh and lustily'.

ASHARD (adj.) ajar.

ASHEN FAGGOT NIGHT Christmas Eve.

ASTORE A phrase added to the end of a statement as *She's gone into the street astore*, in the same way as *'sno* (dost know) is appended in Wiltshire. The two may have some connection.

AVELIN (adj.) silly or stupid. This is a word I received in a short manuscript list, but of which I can find no trace anywhere else.

AYE yes. Used in the northern part of our area in forms which approximate to 'ah'.

BACHE (n.) a hill, a stream valley. Used in Somerset, Wiltshire and

Gloucestershire, especially in place names.

BACKFRIEND (n.) an agnail, a piece of loose skin at the base of a fingernail.

BACK HANDED (adj.) left-handed.

BADGER-PIED (adj.) sandy coloured.

BAIT (n.) food.

BAKER (n.) a woodlouse.

BAL (n.) in the Cornish tin mining industry, a working. *Bal Maidens* were women who worked at ground level.

BANNIS(TICKLE) (n.) a stickleback.

BAMS (n. pl.) gaiters.

BANNUT (n.) a walnut.

BARGE (vb.) to belch.

BARKEN (n.) a farmyard. A form of 'barton'.

BARM (n.) yeast.

BATTER (n.) a railway embankment.

BAVINS (n. pl.) firewood, a rough kind of faggot used in bread ovens.

BEATNESS (n.) fatigue. An unusual combination of two ordinary elements of Standard English.

BECALL (vb.) to scold. *'E becalled I shameful.*

BEDBIND (n.) bindweed. One of the many similar forms for this weed. The first element can also be *Beddy-, Beth-, Betty-* or *Bes*—followed by *Wind* or *Wine* (that is *Wind* with the -d omitted), e.g. *Beddywind* or *Bethwine.*

BEET, BAIT (vb.) to replenish the fire. In fishing communities to mend nets.

BEETLE (n.) a wooden mallet. The head was bound with an iron ring just behind the striking surface. In use, the wood frayed and turned back on the ring, giving the expression 'beetle-browed'.

BELK (vb.) to belch.

BELLOCK (vb.) to bellow. A variant form of the same word.

BELLOWSED OUT (adj.) exhausted.

BELVE (vb.) to bellow (of cows).

BETWIT (vb.) to tease. See also *Twit.*

BIDE (vb.) to stay, the old meaning of 'abide'. The past tense is *Bid*. *'E told I to bide where I were, so I bid there.*

BIRD KEEPING (n.) protecting crops from the depredations of birds. Also called *Bird Starving.*

BIRD'S EYE (n.) Germander Speedwell.

BITBAT (n.) a bat (the mammal).

BIVER (vb.) to quiver, to shiver (of persons). Quivering of the underlip.

BLACKBOB (n.) a beetle.

BLARE (vb.) to bellow (of cows).

BLADDER (n.) a blister.

BLANKERS (n. pl.) sparks.

BLATCH (n.) soot, a smut; (adj.) black, sooty; (vb.) to blacken.

BLEAT (vb.) to moo (of cows). Cornwall. Also found as *Bleak.*

BLEEDING HEARTS (n. pl.) red Wallflowers.

BLINDHOUSE (n.) a lock-up, a name found on the Wiltshire–Somersetshire border. 'Blind' means, in this case, 'windowless'. It has nothing to do with the fact that the majority of their occupants were 'blind-drunk' at the time of their incarceration.

BLUE-VINNIED (adj.) covered with blue mould, as cheese.

BLUNDERSTONE (adj.) clumsy.

BLUSTEROUS (adj.) windy (of weather). Not the usual ending.

BOBBISH (adj.) in good health. Also *Bobbant*, but this can mean, in addition, 'pert' or 'forward' of persons.

BOKE (vb.) to belch, to retch. This is mainly a north-country word which extends into Gloucestershire.

BONNY (n.) a fire (indoors). Used in my family, although I have found no trace of its elsewhere. Presumably connected with 'bonfire'.

BOOSING (n.) a cowshed.

BOTTOM (n.) a river valley, low lying lands. Used in place names.

BRANDS (n. pl.) freckles.

BRAVE (adj.) in good health.

BRAY (vb.) to neigh (of horses).

BRAYING (vb. and n.) in the west-country woollen industry, this term is used for scouring the cloth after it has been woven.

BREAK (vb.) to tear. Used for clothes as in 'My sock is broken' or *I bin a-broke the knee of my trousers*. It is said that *Tear* was used of crockery, etc. as in 'I've tore the plate', but I have never come across this use of the word.

BRICKLE, BRICKLY (adj.) brittle. See *Bruckle, Bruckly*.

BRIZE (vb.) to press down on.

BRUCKLE, BRUCKLY (adj.) brittle. This is a south-western form of the same word. *Bruckle* can also be a verb as in *The bread do bruckle*.

BUCCA (n.) a scarecrow. This word, which originated in the old Cornish language, has many similar and presumably related forms in dialect, such as *Bugabo(o), Bugalo, Buglug*. In R.S., words like 'bogeyman' or 'bugbear' have the meaning of something terrifying. Halliwell defines *Bugabo* as 'a bugbear, a ghost' and adds. 'According to Coles the term fomerly applied to "an ugly, wide-mouthed picture carried about at the May games"'.

BULLYRAG (vb.) to scold, to abuse.

BUNGERSOME (adj.) awkward.

BUNT (vb.) to butt (of cows etc.). Also found as *Bunch* or *Bulk*.

BURNY-BAKE BURNY-BEAT (n. and vb.) burning turf from the surface of a field, so that the ash will increase the fertility. Also known as *Devonshiring* or *Denshering*. *Burny-Bake* has always been used in my experience as a noun, meaning 'bonfire ash'.

BUSSA (n.) salting trough, a bread bin. Cornwall.

BUSSES (n. pl.) ears. Devonshire.

BUSSOCK (vb.) to cough.

BUTT (n.) a paddock, a small plot of land.

BUTTIES (n. pl.) (work)mates.

A BUTTON SHORT not quite right in the head.

CABBY (adj.) sticky. One of a large group of words, similar in form and related in meaning. See a more detailed account under *Clabby*.

CADDLE (vb.) to quarrel, to fight as children often do in a playful manner, but annoying to the parents. As a noun it means difficulty or confusion. A harrassed housewife says that she is in such a caddle, or a skein of wool is in a caddle when it is tangled. Hence *Caddling, Caddlesome* (adj.) annoying or uncertain (of weather).

CADY (n.) the weakest pig of the litter.

CADY (n.) a hat.

CALLY (n.) a sweet. This, and the previous word, I heard when I was young, but I cannot find any other reference to them.

CAM HANDED (adj.) left-handed.

CARRIAGE (n.) an irrigation channel in a water-meadow.

CATCH (vb.) to congeal, to begin to freeze (of water).

CATCHY (adj.) uncertain (of weather).

CATPOLES (n. pl.) tadpoles.

CAVINGS (n. pl.) chaff.

CAVVY (adj.) silly, stupid. A word contained in a short manuscript, which I did not know and which I cannot find in any other source.

CHACKLE (vb.) to gossip.

CHAIN (n.) the warp on a loom (the stationary threads through which the shuttle passes).

CHAM (vb.) to chew. A form of 'champ'.

CHAMBER (n.) a bedroom. Still occasionally heard, although now archaic in R.S.

CHARM, CHERM (n.) A loud, confused noise, often used of the singing of birds.

CHATTER MAG (n.) a gossip.

CHILD (n.) still used in its old sense of 'girl', and pronounced cheel. In its more usual meaning, the plural is always *Childern*. In Middle English the plural was 'childer', and then a second plural ending, the old -n, was added. So 'children' is a double plural that has been accepted in our language, the form used in the southwest counties being nearer to the original.

CHILDAGS (n. pl.) chilblains. See *Springdags*.

CHILVER (n.) a ewe lamb. *Chilver Hog* (n.) the same up to the age of two years.

CHIMP (n.) a shoot on a potato, which has to be removed to keep them in good condition.

CHUCKLE HEADED (adj.) foolish.

CHUMP (n.) a log of wood, of a size for putting on the fire.

CLABBY (adj.) sticky. This word occurs in many different forms such as *Cabby, Clammy, Claumy, Clibby, Cleaty, Clutchy* or *Claggy*. The last is said to have in addition the meaning of 'wet' or 'miry'.

CLACKERS, often *A Pair of Clackers* (n.) a rattle for bird-scaring. A form of the word 'clappers'. When I was young it meant two pieces of flat bone or wood held loosely between the fingers, and rattled rhythmically in the manner of castanets.

CLAM, CLAMMER (n.) a footbridge. Devonshire.

CLATTY, CLATTED, CLITTY (adj.) tangled.

CLAUSEN (adj.) flagged (of floor). Devonshire.

CLAVEL, CLAVY (n.) the mantelpiece. Strictly speaking, the clavy is the beam supporting the opening of the fireplace, and the mantelpiece should be *Clavy Tack* (*Tack* = shelf), but it is usually refered to simply as the *Clavy*.

CLAY (n.) a *Clay*, a children's marble made of clay.

CLEATY (adj.) sticky. See *Clabby*.

CLEEVE (adj.) steep. Often used in place names.

CLICK-, CLICKY-HANDED (adj.) left-handed.

CLIDE (n.) gossegrass. This word turns up in several different forms, some singular, some plural; *Cliders, Clites, Clivers, Clives, Cly,* all related, it seems, to *Cleavers*, a name for the plant in fairly general use.

CLINKER, CLINKERBELL (n.) icicle. See *Conkerbell*.

CLINEY (adj.) unwell. Obviously related to the phrase 'to go into a decline', one of the not very clear cut illnesses of former times.

CLIT (adj.) matted, often used of soil.

CLITES (n.) See *Clide*.

CLIVERS (n.) See *Clide*.

CLOAM (n.), CLOAMEN (adj.) earthenware. Devonshire, Cornwall and west Somersetshire.

CLUMBERSOME (adj.) awkward.

CLUMBLE FISTED (adj.) clumsy.

CLUMPER (vb.) to walk heavily, to stumble.

CLY (n.) See *Clide*.

COLLY COW (n.) a ladybird.

COMICAL (adj.) awkward of character, a comical person makes himself as awkward as possible.

CONIGRE (n.) a rabbit warren. Only used in place names.

CONKERBELL (n.) icicle. Also found as *Cocklebell*. See *Clinkerbell*.

COOCKY-HANDED (adj.) left-handed.

COSTERIL (n.) a container used to take drink to the harvest fields. See *Plough Bottle*.

COUCH (vb.) to sit, settle down. Used as in the sentence *You couch down there and wait for I*. Pronounced 'cooch'.

COUPY (n.) a chicken. A children's word. Also a *Coupy Egg*.

COUPY (vb.) to crouch. A form of the more usual *Croupy*.

COW CLAT (n.) a patch of cow dung.

COWFLOP, COWSLOP (n.) a cowslip.

CRATCH (n.) a hayrack. An old word, still used in Gloucestershire.

CRIB (n.) a snack, food taken to the fields by farm workers.

CROOGER (n.) a woodlouse.

CROUPY, COUPY DOWN (vb.) to crouch.

CROW, PIGS' CROW (n.) a pigstye. Cornwall.

CRUST (n.) a snack, food taken to the fields by farm workers.

CUNNY-HANDED (adj.) left-handed.

CUTTY (n.) a wren.

DACK (n.) a weakling pig.

DADDOCK (n.) rotten wood. Hence *Daddocky* (adj.) rotten.

DAGGLED (adj.) exhausted. Gloucestershire. Also found as *Dagged* or *Duggled*.

DAGGLER, DAGLET or even DAGGER (n.) icicle.

DALLPIG (n.) a weakling pig.

DAP (vb.) to brand sheep. Perhaps a form of 'dab'.

DAP (vb.) to bounce (a ball). Also used as a noun.

DAP (vb.) to go. The word implies a short distance, 'Just dap over the shop and get some vinegar', or quick motion, 'He soon dapped down the pub and bought some beer'.

DAPS (n.) the very image of, as in 'He's the very daps of his father'.

DAPS (n. pl.) plimsoles.

DARLING, DARREL (n.) a weakling pig.

DEDDICKIE (n.) a gipsy.

DELIRIOUS TREMOR (n. pl.) the 'shakes', a distortion of 'delirium tremens', putting it in a more familiar form.

DEVONSHIRE, DENSHER (vb.) paring off the top layer of turf in a field, and burning it in order to enrich the soil with ash. See *Burny-Bake*.

DEWBIT (n.) a snack eaten in the fields by farm workers. The time of eating and the composition varied, but it was especially associated with the long hours of work during the corn or hay harvest.

DIGGLE (vb.) to grow abundantly. Also *Diggles* (n.) an abundance, as in

Let's go blackerrying, there's diggles on 'em.

DILLER (n.) a shaft horse. See *Thiller.*

DILLING (n.) a weakling pig.

DILLS (n. pl.) the shafts of a cart. See *Thills.*

DILLY (n.) a duck. A children's word.

DIMMET, DIMPSEY (n.) twilight.

DISREMEMBER (vb.) to forget. Two ordinary elements put together to produce a new word.

DODDER, DUDDER (vb.) to bewilder a person, to confuse him in an argument. *All in a Dudder* quite bewildered.

DOGSMOUTH (n.) an antirrhinum in the garden, yellow toadflax in the wild.

DORREL (n.) a weakling pig.

DOUT (vb.) to extinguish. An old word, still used in the south-west.

DRAM (n.) a swath of hay. Cornwall.

DRAWN (n.) the channel in a water meadow which takes water back to the stream.

DRIPPLES (n. pl.) the sides of a waggon. See *Thripples.*

DROCK (n.) a drain under a road. Still used in official documents.

DRUNG, DRANG, DRONG (n.) a passageway, usually between buildings. Sometimes *Drangway.*

DRYTH (n.) drought.

DUB (vb.) to throw. Halliwell defines it as 'to strike a cloth with teasels to raise the nap'.

DUDDEKIN (n.) an earth closet, a lavatory.

DUDMAN (n.) a scarecrow. Also someone shabbily dressed.

DUMBLE, DUMMEL (adj.) stupid.

DUMMOCK (n.) a cow.

DUNCH (adj.) deaf. See *Dunny.*

DUNCHED (adj.) cramped. One is 'all dunched up' after, say, a long drive in a car. Also heavy (of bread). Hence *Dunch Dumpling* which is made of flour and water.

DUNNEKIN, DUNNICK (n.) an earth closet, a lavatory.

DUNNY (adj.) deaf. See *Dunch.*

DURNS (n. pl.) door jambs.

DUSTMAN (n.) the rustic equivalent of the Sandman, who lulls children to sleep.

DYKE (n.) an earth closet, a lavatory.

EASS (n.) an earthworm. See also *Yess.*

EDDER (n.) a hazel wand for keeping a laid hedge in place. See *Ether.*

EGGLES, EGGLETS, EGLONS (n. pl.) haws.

EKKYMOWL (n.) a bat (mammal). Cornwall.

ELMS (n. pl.) bundles of straw of straw for thatching. See also *Yealms.*

EMMET (n.) an ant. A form of the Anglo-Saxon word 'æmete', which is also the root of the word 'ant' itself.

EMPT (vb.) to empty. This word has lost its -y possibly by being mistakenly construed as a 'free infinitive'.

EMPTING CLOAM (vb.) getting drunk. Devonshire.

ERDING (n.) a metathesised form of *Redding*, red dye. See *Reddle.*

ERRISH (n.) a stubble field. See *Arrish.*

ETHER (n.) a wand, usually of hazel, either woven in and out of the top of a wattle fence, or used to keep the branches of a laid hedge in place.

An eldern stake and a blackthorn ether
Will make a hedge to last for ever.

(West country saying)

ETTLE (n.) a nettle. By metanalysis, a nettle becomes an *Ettle*. (Metanalysis is mistaken division.)

EVET (n.) a newt. In this case the word in Standard English was formed by metanalysis—an evet became a nevet, a newt.

EVIL (n.) a dung fork.

Because of the voicing of initial f, i.e. pronouncing the f at the beginning of words as v, it is often difficult to know under which of these letters to include dialect terms. On the whole, those which show any connection with R.S. words beginning with f are listed here.

FAGGOT (n.) a bundle, whether it was of firewood or of pig's liver, with breadcrumbs and seasoning, wrapped in 'caul fat'. It is also used for a woman in a more or less critical sense, 'silly old faggot'. Pronounced 'fakket'.

FAIRY (n.) a weasel. Somersetshire.

FANCY MAN (n.) a woman's lover.

FANTAIG (n.) a fluster. *Now dwon't 'ee get in sich a fantaig.*

FENNY (adj.) mouldy. More often *Vinny*, as in *Blue-Vinnied* cheese.

FEWSTER (vb.) to fester.

FIGS (n. pl.) raisins. Hence *Figgy Pudding* or *Figgety Duff*, suet pudding made with dried fruit.

FILLER (n.) a shaft horse. The same as *Diller* or *Thiller*.

FILLERS (n. pl.) the shafts of a waggon.

FIRK (n.) something or someone small. In my grandmother's speech, things that could be expected to be small were 'little grigs', so that when she was peeling potatoes, she might say 'I be nearly finished, I only got the grigs to do'. But *Firk* was a term of reproach, 'What a little firk he is'.

FITCH, FITCHEW, FITCHY (n.) a polecat. Devonshire and Cornwall.

FITCH (vb.) to flick.

FLABBER (vb.) to eat greedily.

FLAKE (n.) a substantial hurdle.

FLAM NEW, FLAME NEW (adj.) brand new.

FLARE (n.) fat, from around the pig's kidneys usually. Also found as *Flay* or *flead*.

FLASK (n.) a clothes *Flask*—a clothes basket.

FLECK, FLICK (n.) fat from a pig.

FLEET (n.) urine.

FLITMOUSE, FLITTERMOUSE (n.) a bat (mammal).

FLITTERS (n.) smithereens, tatters. A plate can be broken 'all to flitters'. Also found as flittereens.

FLOATING MEADOW (n.) a water-meadow, irrigated by a system of carriages and drawns.

FLUMP (vb.) to flop down. 'She flumped in the chair.' Also as it 'It fell down flump'.

FOGGER (n.) a cowman. Originally, a groom, who also fed the cows.

FORESPUR (n.) a hock of pork.

FRAME (n.) skeleton, the bones of a chicken that has been eaten.

FROARED (adj.) cold (of persons).

FUDDECKING (vb.) fidgeting. Probably a distortion of the same word.

FURMITY (n.) the drink usually known as frumenty, from Latin 'frumentum', corn, French 'froment', wheat. This is not confined to the south-west, but it plays an important part in Hardy's *The Mayor of Casterbridge*. It is made by simmering wheat grains in water until they are soft, then putting in a quantity of dried fruit and yeast. Milk, and alcohol in the form of cider or sherry, could be added if desired.

GAIT (n.) a mannerism, a way of walking. *What a silly gait you've got into.*

GALLER, GALLOW, GALLY (vb.) to be frightened. *I were gallered to death.* Hence *Gallibagger, gallicrow* (n.) a scarecrow.

GAMMY (adj.) sticky.

GAMMY-HANDED (adj.) left-handed.

GAPESNATCH (n.) a fool. Used as a mild form of abuse. *You girt gapesnatch, you.* Older sources give *Gapesnest* 'raree shrew', 'a gaping stock'.

GAUGE BRICK (n.) a brick which was put in the oven, and which showed, by its change of colour, when this correct temperature had been reached.

GAWK (n.) an awkward, clumsy person.

GAY (adj.) in good health.

GEEK (vb.) to peep. Cornwall.

GEMINI this word is used as an exclamation, expressing mild surprise. It is the Latin for 'twins', and refers to Castor and Pollux, the heavenly twins, one of the signs of the Zodiac.

GIBBLES (n. pl.) onions of varying sorts, either spring onions, or those 'grown from bulbs' (Goddard and Dartnell).

GIN (vb.) to begin. This form was used by the Bristol poet, Chatterton; *In virgine, the sweltry sun gan sheen.*

GIPSY NUTS (n. pl.) hips and haws.

GLADDIGOASTER (n.) a woodlouse.

GLUTCH (vb.) to swallow. It is said, in some books, that to *Glutch* is to swallow with difficulty, while to *Quilt*

means to swallow in the ordinary way. In my experience we only use word *Glutch* for swallowing of any kind, although if one had a sore throat, one might say *I do find it hard to glutch.*

GLUTCH (vb.) to belch. Gloucestershire.

GOAT (vb.) to stook, to stand sheaves in piles to dry.

GOGGLE (vb.) to drink avidly. Also found as *Golk, Guddle* and *Guggle*.

GOLDEN CHAIN (n.) laburnum.

GRAIN (n.) a tine of a gardening or hay fork. The fork is usually called a *Prong*, so a hay fork is a 'two-grained prong'.

GRAMFER (n.) a very common form of 'grandfather'.

GRAMFER (n.) a woodlouse.

GRAMMER (n.) a form of 'grandmother'. Now almost obsolete.

GRAVELWIND (n.) bindweed.

GRAVES (n. pl.) scraps of meat left when fat has been rendered.

GRIG (n.) something small. See *Firk*.

GRIGGLES (n. pl.) small apples left on the tree. Boys were allowed, by custom, to knock them down. This was called *Griggling* or *Apple-Owling*.

GRISKIN (n.) a cut of pork, the loin.

GRIGLANDS (n.) heather. Cornwall.

GROUNDLILY (n.) bindweed.

GROUNDS (n. pl.) fields.

GRUTS (n. pl.) tea leaves left in the pot after the tea has been poured. This word occurs in forms, such as *Grounds, Grouts, Greets* and *Groushans*. (The latter is a Cornish word.) The meaning usually involves something like spent tea leaves— grains of oats or the last wort to be run from beer.

GULLET (n.) a puddle. Sometimes a

stream or drainhole.

GUSS (n.) the saddle girth. In the Somerset coal field the *Guss and Crook* was used to haul trams of coal. It consisted of a leather belt round a boy's waist and a chain, attached to the front, and which ended in a hook. The chain and hook passed through the boy's legs as he advanced in a stooping position.

H being so frequently dropped, it is difficult to know whether to list words here, or according to the first vowel. Those which seem to be connected with words in Standard English beginning with h are to be found here.

HACKLING (vb.) coughing. One of many similar words. See under *Hasking.*

HAGS, HAGAGS (n. pl.) haws.

HAIRIF (n.) goosegrass.

HALLEGE (n.) fuss, disorder, confusion.

HALSE (n.) hazel. Perhaps a metathesised form.

HAMS (n. pl.) low-lying meadow lands, generally in the curves of a river.

HANDPAT (adv.) within reach. *I had my scissors handpat.*

HANDY (prep.) near. *My house is handy the shops.*

HARLED (adj.) tangled. Perhaps a form of 'whorled'. HARL can be used as a verb to mean putting one leg of a dead rabbit through the other in order to carry it more easily.

HARVEST ROW (n.) a shrew mouse.

HASK (vb.) to cough. This word is used most frequently in the present participle, *Hasking*, and occurs in a number of forms: *Hackling, Hisking, Hassocking, Hauking, Hecketing,* all

with related meanings, such as 'hoarse', 'choked with phlegm'. Probably connected with the Standard English word 'hacking' as in a 'hacking cough'.

HATCH (n.) a line of hay waiting to be 'pooked' (made into piles).

HAWBERRIES (n. pl.) haws.

HAZZLED (adj.) chapped.

HEAVE (vb.) to sweat (of pavements, etc.) in humid weather. *Heavy* (adj.) pronounced 'heevy', damp. One can say 'heaving with damp'.

HEDDLE (n.) the wire that connects the harness in a loom with the threads of the warp.

HEFT (vb.) to test for weight. See also *Teft.*

HEN AND CHICKEN (n.) the flower London Pride.

HENGE, HANGE (n.) the heart, liver and lights of a pig, or less often a sheep, attached to the windpipe and formerly hung on a rail in butchers' shops.

HEN-TOED (adj.) pigeon toed.

HILE (vb.) the usual west-country word for 'stooking' or 'shocking', that is picking up sheaves of corn after it has been cut, and standing them in groups to dry.

HILT (n.) a young sow.

HIND (n.) a bailiff. Devonshire and Cornwall.

HODMADOD (n.) a scarecrow.

HOOSET (n.) a noisy demonstration expressing disapproval of misconduct in marriage. See also *Rough Music* and *Skimmety Ride.*

HOOZLED (adj.) hoarse.

HORCH (vb.) to butt (of cows).

HOUND (n.) the forepart of a waggon.

HOUSEWALLAH (n.) someone who lives in a house. This word, quoted by Sir

W. H. Cope in *Hampshire Words and Phrases*, published by the English Dialect Society in 1883, is a Romany word. It is earlier than all the other '-wallah' words picked up in India by our troops there, and reminds us that Romany is originally an Indian language. I very much doubt whether it was ever much used by dialect speakers, but it is included here because of its intrinsic interest.

HOWK (vb.) to root about in the ground with the snout as pigs do. Perhaps a form of 'hook'. See *Uck*.

HUMMOCK (n.) a cow. See *Dummock*.

HUNCH (vb.) to butt (of cows etc.).

HUNCH (n.) a hunk.

HUNGERED (adj.) hungry. An old form still current in Cornwall.

HUSBIRD (n.) a term of reproach. See *Whizbird*.

HUTCH (n.) a bin. Cornwall.

ICECANDLES (n.) icicle. Also found as *Icedaggle, Icelet*, and *Icybell*.

ISS (n.) earthworm. See *eass*.

JIBBER (n.) a restless horse.

JIMMINY a form of the exclamation *Gemini*.

JONNICK honest(ly). A children's word used when attesting the truth of what has been said.

JOEY (n.) a weakling pig.

JOEY (n.) an old silver threepennybit. Also anything bright, such as the reflection that a small, hand-held mirror makes on a wall.

JUMBLIES (n. pl.) sweets.

KECK (vb.) to retch.

KECKER (n.) the throat, windpipe.

KECK-, KEGGY-, KLECKY-HANDED (adj.) left-handed.

KLUNKER (n.) the windpipe. Cornwall.

KNAP (n.) a little hill.

KNICKY (adj.) in good health.

KNOTLING (n.) Chitterlings, or that part of chitterlings made from the intestine.

LADY COW (n.) ladybird.

LAGGED OUT (adj.) exhausted, tired.

LATTERLAMMAS (n.) an unpunctual or procrastinating person. *Latterlamsical* (adj.) unpunctual, procrastinating. Latterlammas is the Day of Judgement, so this is a person who puts off decisions until that date.

LATTYPRACK (adj.) paralytic. A distortion.

LAUNDER (n.) guttering to take rainwater. Cornwall.

LAWRENCE. A sprite, claimed by many parts of the south-west, and dedicated to indolence. 'To have a touch of the Lawrence', is to be not overfond of work.

LEAR, LEARY (adj.) hungry, empty (of stomach). I have heard it used in special ways, such as the empty feeling after being sick or even meaning 'thirsty' as in *I be main lear for a cup of tea*.

LEASE (vb.) to glean, to pick up the ears of corn accidentally left after the harvest has been carted. *Leasings* (n. pl.) ears so collected.

LEW (adj.) warm. Used in *Lew-Warm* (luke-warm).

LEWTH (n.) warmth.

LEWZE (n.) pig sty.

LIMBER (n.) a shaft of a cart.

LINEPOST (n.) clothes post.

LINHAY (n.) a cartshed.

LIPPING (adj.) wet, stormy, showery (of weather).

LISSOM (adj.) active, lively (especially of children).

LIST (n.) the selvedge of a woven cloth.

LITTON (n.) a churchyard. The first part is the Anglo-Saxon word 'lic', meaning *body* or *corpse*, the second means *enclosure* (a common element in place names). Related words are 'lych gate', where the priest joined the waiting corpse, and the now obsolete 'leech-way', the churchyard path.

LIVERSICK (n.) an agnail, a loose piece of skin at the base of a fingernail.

LONDON YORKS (n. pl.) straps, or just pieces of string, fastened around the trousers just below the knees, to keep the bottoms from trailing in the mud. Usually known as just *Yorks*.

LOLLUP (vb.) to laze, to loll about.

LOOKSEE (vb.) a form of 'look', as in 'Looksee at 'en standing' there'. Always used as an imperative, i.e. a 'command'. In dialect, we often use a pronoun with the imperative as in 'Sit 'ee down there', and this may be that pronoun turned into a more familiar form, or at least one that seems logically connected with the verb; or it could be a 'free infinitive' (see chapter 4), with the same change, i.e. 'Looky at 'en' becomes 'Looksee at 'en'.

LOP (vb.) to idle about. Also found as *Loppet*. Hence *Loppus* (n.) an idler. The last word is usually used as a term of abuse.

LOUCH (vb.) to slouch. Dialect sometimes adds an -s to the beginning of words, and occasionally takes one off, which rightly belongs there.

LOVE-A-LIDO (n.) One of the many cor-ruptions of the flower name, Love-in Idleness, the wild pansy. *Love-an'- Idols, Loving-Idols* and *Nuffin-Idols* are also found.

LUG (n.) a rod, pole or perch, i.e. $5\frac{1}{2}$ yards. I have only ever heard it used as square measure, i.e. $30\frac{1}{4}$ sq. yards. The standard allotment measured 'ten lug', no -s being added for the plural.

MAG (n.) prattle. MAGGER (n.) a gossip. Also found as *Chatter-Mag*.

MAID, MAIDEN (n.) a girl. Among older dialect speakers, the word 'girl' is little used, these two words and *Wench* taking its place.

MAIN (adv.) very, as in 'That were main teart' (that was very painful). *A Main Few* means a large number.

MAMMET (n.) a scarecrow.

MALBOROUGH-HANDED (adj.) left-handed, or awkward in the use of tools. This unfortunate reputation of the natives of Marlborough goes back a long way. Walter Map (c. 1140– c.1209), an Anglo-Saxon ecclesiastic, who wrote 'De Nugis Curialum' (Of Courtiers' trifles), a collection of anecdotes throwing light on the reign of Henry II, says, 'If one is faulty in his use of this tongue, we say that he speaketh French of Marlborough'.

MAUND (n.) a basket. Various kinds of basket are stipulated as the only one that can be called by this name, but they are usually associated with food, e.g. a chaff basket for feeding horses, or a basket with a double lid used for carrying food to the harvest fields.

MAWKIN (n.) a scarecrow. Also a bunch of rags attached to a stick, used for cleaning out of an oven the ashes of the sticks burnt in it to heat it.

MAZED (adj.) mad. Devonshire.

MAYBERRIES (n. pl.) haws.

MAZZARD (n.) the head, the hair. *I be going to get my mazzard cut.*

MEGRIMS (n.) headache, depression. A distortion of 'migraine'.

MIDSTAY, MIDSTEAD (n.) the threshing floor in a barn.

MIFF (vb.) to take offence.

MILLARD (n.) a miller. Note the excrescent -d.

MIN used as in *they'll let thee have it, min, when they do see thee* always with a rather threatening tone.

MIND (vb.) to remember. *I do mind when I were young.*

MOKUS (n.) a donkey.

MOOT (n.) a root, tree stump.

MOP (n.) a tuft of grass.

MORE (n.) a root, tree stump or the plant itself, as in a 'strawberry more'.

MOUCH (vb.) to pilfer out of doors as, for example, boys stealing apples from orchards.

MOUSESNAP, MOUSESNATCH (n.) a mousetrap.

MOW (n.) a rick or stack. Often given a specialised meaning such as a straw rick as opposed to a hay rick. This use is common in Gloucestershire, Devonshire and Cornwall. In other parts of the south-west, *Mow* refers to the space at either end of the barn, where the corn was stored to await threshing. The centre, the threshing floor is known as the *Midstay* or *Midstead.*

MOWYARD (n.) a rickyard, stackyard.

MUNGE (vb.) to chew. A form of 'munch'. A child, who tended to swallow its food whole was told to *munge it like a bunny.*

MURFLES (n. pl.) freckles. Devonshire and Cornwall.

MURYAN (n.) ant. Cornwall. A survival of a an old Cornish word.

NAILSPRING (n.) an agnail.

NAMMET (n.) one of the snacks that farm workers took with them into the fields, especially at harvest time. The origin of this word is 'noon meat', but the time at which it was eaten varied considerably.

NAN? What did you say? Said by someone who has not heard or not understood what has been said.

NAPKNEED (adj.) knockneed.

NEALD (n.) a needle. A metathesised form.

NESSOCK (n.) a donkey. Gloucestershire.

NESTLE-TRIPE (n.) One of the many words used to describe the weakest pig in a litter. Also found as *Nestle-Draf, Nestle-Drish, Nestle-Drudge* and *Nestle-Bird.* In addition, the first element may be *Nuzzle-.*

NIDDICK (n.) the neck. Devonshire and Cornwall.

NIMPINGANG (n.) a whitlow. Devonshire and Cornwall.

NIRRUP (n.) a donkey.

NIDDY-NODDY (n.) the tremors.

NIT (conj.) nor yet. *I ain't got no job, nit no money.*

NOTHERING (vb.) trembling.

NUNCH (n.) the mid-morning snack. Also known as *Lunch.*

NURK (n.) See *Runt.*

NUTTER (vb.) to whinny (of horses). Gloucestershire.

OAKSEY LILY (n.) the snake's head fritillary.

OAVES (n. pl.) the eaves of a house.

OOZLE (n.) the throat. Cornwall.

OOZLING (vb.) wheezing.

OOZED (adj.) hoarse.

OPEWAY (n.) a passageway,

OVERRIGHT (prep.) opposite.

PAIR OF TRUCKS (n. s.) a handbarrow, with big wheels, such as decorators used before the war. Now that these have disappeared, the expression is only found in a *Pair of Sack Trucks*.

PAKE (n.) a hand. Used in the phrase 'I can't wait to get my pakes on it'.

PANE (n.) the palm of the hand. Devonshire.

PANTERNY (n.) a pantry. A distortion.

PARKY (adj.) chilly (of weather).

PARROCK (n.) a paddock.

PEART (adj.) impertinent, lively, in good health. Probably a form of 'pert'.

PEEPSHOW (n.) flowers placed between a piece of cardboard and a piece of glass, the edges being bound with tape.

PELCH (vb.) to butt (of cows).

PIDDLE (n.) a paddock.

PIGBERRIES, PIGHALES, PIGSHELLS (n. pl.) haws.

PIGMEAT (n.) In the west country, a distinction is still sometimes made between 'pork', the meat from a young pig, and 'pig meat' from a fully grown one.

PINE (n.) a cowshed. The p sometimes produces a w, so giving the pronunciation 'pwine'.

PINSWELL (n.) a boil. Pronounced 'pinsle'.

PIN-TOED (adj.) pigeon-toed.

PISSABED (n.) a dandelion. Widely considered a remedy for bed wetting. Cf. French *pissenlit*.

PITCH (vb.) to make a path with small, uneven stones called *Pitchin*, placed on edge, snow is said to *Pitch* when it settles on the ground.

PITCH (n.) a steep hill.

PITCHPOLL head over heels.

PITH (n.) the crumb of the loaf.

PLAT (n.) a paddock or small enclosed place. Sometimes used in place names e.g. 'Brickplat'.

PLAT (n.) the plain of the downs in Wiltshire.

PLIM (vb.) to swell. Doors are said to *Plim* when they swell with damp and are difficult to open.

PLOCK (n.) a log of wood for the fire.

PLOUGH BOTTLE (n.) a container, not necessarily a bottle, in which drink was carried to the fields by farm workers. See also *Costeril*.

PLUMP (n.) a pump. A common distortion.

POG (vb.) to thrust something in, such as a dibber when planting potatoes or a carpet needle through the canvas base.

POGGER (n.) a garden dibber.

POHEAD (n.) a tadpole.

POKE (n.) Calves' poke is the calves' stomach, a source of rennet for cheese making. *Poke* is an old word for a bag.

POOK (n.) a haycock. *Pook* (vb.) to make hay into cocks.

POPPY (n.) a sweet. A children's word.

POT, PUT(T) (n.) a two-wheeled tipping cart. Manure was formerly carried to the fields in a pair of pots, slung across a horse's back, and the term was transferred to the cart with the same use.

PRAIL (n.) three playing-cards of the same value, but different suits.

PRONG (n.) a fork for digging, or a hayfork.

PUFFS (n. pl.) firewood.

PUD, PUDDY (n.) the hand. A children's word.

PUGGLED (adj.) stupid.

PUMPLE-FOOTED (adj.) club-footed, pigeon-toed.

PURDLE (vb.) to *Purdle* along is to go at a good speed. Also to fall headlong. Probably the word 'purl' with an excrescent d.

PURRED, PURREYED (adj.) rotten. Perhaps a distortion of 'perished'.

PUT, PUTT (n.) See *Pot*.

PUZZIVANT (n.) a fluster. 'He put I in such a puzzivant'. The word is said to come from the French 'poursuivant', a follower. In a note to chapter XVII of *The Astonishing History of Troy Town*, Sir Arthur Quiller-Couch explains it originated from the contempt with which the west-country sea-captains treated the poursuivants sent down by Edward IV to threaten his displeasure.

QUAILAWAY (n.) a sty on the eye. Devonshire and Cornwall.

QUAR (n.) a quarry. (vb.) to work as a quarryman. This word has probably lost its ending by being mistakenly construed as a 'free infinitive'. (See chapter 4).

QUAT (vb.) to squat, or more commonly, to sit *You quat down there and drink this tea*. This is the word 'squat', which has lost its s.

QUILL (n.) the bobbin in the shuttle of a loom, which carries the thread of the weft. *Quill-Winding* (n.) the operation of loading the bobbins. Also *Quill-Winder*.

QUILT (vb.) to swallow. See *Glutch*.

QUILTER (n.) the throat.

QUIRK (vb.) to complain.

RAFTY, RASTY RUSTY (adj.) rancid (of bacon). The word I knew was *Rufty*, a general word of disapproval, probably from association with 'rough'. *He were wearing a rufty old coat*.

RAMBLERS (n. pl.) potatoes, grown from those of last year's crop accidentally left in the ground.

RAMES (n.) a skeleton, a very thin person.

RANGLE (vb.) to twine around something as a climbing plant does.

RANT (vb.) to tear (n.) a tear. *You bin a-ranted your trousers*. Also as a verb, to do something, something impatiently, especially taking off clothes.

RAVEL-BACK (n.) an agnail. See *Rebble-Back*.

REAM (n.) cream.

REDDLE, RUDDLE (n.) red dye, used for marking sheep or getting a flat surface on a millstone. Also *Redding* and *Erding*.

REAP-HOOK (n.) a sickle. Pronounced 'rip-hook'. This tool is to be distinguished from the old sickle which had a shorter, serrated blade (see SHEKEL). The *Reap-Hook* is often called a *Bagging-Hook* or a *Fagging-Hook*.

REAR-MOUSE (n.) a bat (mammal). Also found as *Airy-Mouse, Rennie-Mouse* or *Rye-Mouse*.

REED-BIND (n.) bindweed.

RINNICK (n.) See RUNT.

ROLLER (n.) a line of hay waiting to be *Pooked*.

ROUGH (adj.) ill, unwell.

ROUGH MUSIC (n.) An impromptu 'serenade', produced on pans, saucepan lids etc., which shows disapproval of the conduct of a partner in a marriage (infidelity, wife beating or nagging). See *Hooset* and *Skimmety Ride*.

RUDDER (n.) a sieve (vb.) to sieve. The implement referred to is a big sieve used to sift ashes or corn. This is a form of the Standard English word 'riddle'.

RUNT (n.) the smallest pig in a litter. Usually found in such forms as *Rinnick* or *Nurk*. This last is a metathesised form.

RUTCHY (adj.) rancid (of bacon).

S being frequently voiced at the beginning of a word, i.e. pronounced as z, it is sometimes difficult to know where to list dialect words, under S or under Z. On the whole, I have chosen S, as this is more in keeping with English spelling.

ST FIFER'S DANCE, ST VIPER'S DANCE (n.) St Vitus' Dance. These are distortions, producing more easily recognisable forms.

a-SAM (adj.) ajar (of a door).

SAIL (n.) the upright spar of a hurdle.

SAR (vb.) to feed animals. A form of 'serve'. Also *Sarren* (n.) a helping.

SCAG (vb.) to tear (n.) a tear. Used of a small tear caused, for instance, by barbed wire.

SCALLYWAP (n.) a barber. Used only in my family, as far as I know.

SCAUTER (vh.) to go at a rapid pace. *They were scautering along.*

SCOOCHY-HANDED (adj.) left-handed. A sibilated form of COOCHY-HANDED.

SCOTH (n.) a chink, a narrow opening between boards.

SCRAMMED (adj.) very cold (of people). See *Shrammed.*

SCRAM-, SCRAMMY-HANDED (adj.) left-handed.

SCRAMMISH, SCRAMMY (adj.) clumsy.

SCRATCHINGS (n. pl.) scraps of meat left when fat is rendered.

SCREW(EL) (n.) a shrew mouse.

SCROBBLE (vb.) to creep. Gloucestershire. This word turns up in Wiltshire as SCRABBLE, meaning 'to hurry'.

SCROOP (vb.) to creak.

SCROW-LEGGED (adj.) bow-legged.

SCRUMP (vb.) to crunch. This is a sibilated form of a more widespread word 'crump'.

SCRUNCH (vb.) to crunch. Another sibilated word.

SCUD, SKAT (n.) a sudden, sharp shower.

SCUG, SCUGGY (n.) a squirrel. See *Sqwug.*

SCURF (n.) dandruff.

SEG, SIG (n.) urine. Mainly urine collected for use in cloth mills for scouring cloth. The collection was made by the SEG CART, which went around from house to house, and to public houses and workhouses.

SETTLY, SETTY (adj.) bad (of eggs).

SHACKLE (vb.) to walk quickly, sometimes in a shambling sort of way. Like a good many dialect words, often used rather jocularly. *You should a' seen her shackling along.*

SHARD (n.) a gap in a hedge.

SHARPS (n. pl.) the shafts of a cart.

SHEAR-CROP (n.) a shrew mouse.

SHEKEL (n.) the old sickle, with a serrated blade, now replaced by the *Bagging Hook.* See *Reap-Hook.*

SHERRY (n.) a shrew mouse.

SHIPPON (n.) a cowshed.

SHIRP (vb.) to cut off small pieces, as when sharpening a pencil, to whittle.

SHITABED (n.) a dandelion.

SHITSACK (n.) an oak-apple.

SHITSACK DAY (n.) Oak-apple day, King Charles' day, 29 May.

SHRO-CROTCH (n.) a shrew mouse.

SHOOT (n.) the guttering on a house, or, more properly, the downpipe. One can often tell that it is raining at night as one can hear 'the shoots running'.

SHOOT (n.) the weft in a loom.

SHRAMMED (adj.) chilled to the bone, very cold (of persons). Also found as *Scrammed* and *Srammed*.

SHRIGGLE (vb.) to take a last picking of, for example, peas or apples. Also found as *Scriggle* and related to *Griggle*, knocking small apples from trees.

SHRIMPY (adj.) cold.

SHUDDERED (adj.) cold.

SHUTTLE (adj.) active (of children).

SIG (n.) See *Seg*.

SINK (n.) a drain outside, such as the drains in the road. Also the 'swallow holes' into which streams disappear on chalk, to follow an underground course, before reappearing when geological conditions change.

SKIFFLE-, SKIFFY-, SKIVVY-, SQUIFFY-, SQUIPPY-SQUIVER-HANDED (adj.) left-handed.

SKILLIN, SKILLING (n.) a cowshed, often lean-to, with one side open. Also found as *Skeeling* and *Sheeling*. Use of this word is now confined to Wiltshire.

SKIMMINGTON, SIMMETY RIDE (n.) a communal expression of disapproval of conduct in marriage. See *Hooset* and *Rough Music*.

SKINGER (n.) a miser.

SKIVVY-HANDED (adj.) See *Skiffle-handed*.

SLAMMOCK (n.) a slattern. This word occurs in a number of forms, always expressing disapproval, e.g. *Slummicky* (adj.) clumsy, *Slummicking* or *Slammicking* (vb.) slouching. Connected with this group may be also *Slimmix*, a jocular term of abuse. I have heard, for instance 'Come on, slimmix, you got to go out' said to a cat. Another, rather different word is *Slinx* (n.) which is used when speaking of someone, not when addressing them.

SLOBBER (vb.) to guzzle.

SLOOM (vb.) to walk deliberately slowly, to dawdle. Always has overtones of disapproval.

SLUB (n.) wet, loose mud. Hampshire.

SMAAM, SMARM (vb.) to dirty with mud or some such liquid substance. Hair is said to be *smaamed down* by the application of large quantities of grease or hair oil.

SMATCH (n.) taste. A form of 'smack' in the sense of 'It smacks of . . .'.

SMEECH (n.) smoke, soot, dirt. The meaning of this word varies considerably, often being specialised as, for instance, the soot left by smoke on the ceiling.

SNAIL CREEPER (n.) the gathering on a smock.

SNOWELL (n.) a hunk as in 'a girt *Snowell* of bread'. Sometimes confused with STOWELL, a stump, a root, a form of 'stool'.

SOBBING WET (adj.) soaked. This bears a strong resemblance to 'sopping wet' of Standard English, but various other forms occur, e.g. *Sobbed Out* (adj.) boggy (of land), *Sobble* (vb.) to soak, *Sobbled* soaked. Also found is *Sogging Wet*, perhaps a variant of 'soaking' itself.

SOCE a form of address, 'Friends', used by, say, a farmer, addressing his workmen, or to the company in general in a public house. Probably it is a relic of the Latin 'socii', friends, used by mediaeval preachers in their sermons.

SOLE (n.) a wooden plough. See *Sully*.

SOMEWHEN (adv.) sometime. This particular word did not catch on in English, although the similar compound 'somewhere' did. However it is much used in dialect.

SPECKLES (n. pl.) freckles.

SPICK (n.) a thatching spar, a hazel rod, bent into a U shape and used to hold down the 'elms', the bundles of straw.

SPILE (n.) vegetable matter found in wool.

SPLASH (vb.) to plash, to pleach, to weave twigs and branches in and out to make or renew a hedge. This is a sibillated form.

SPLAT (n.) a paddock. A sibillated form of the dialect word *Plat*.

SPRAYED (adj.) chapped, roughened with cold. Usually used of the hands. This word has other forms: *Spree'd, Spreethed, Spreeved, Spreezed*.

SPRINGDAG (n.) a chilblain.

SPRODDLE (vb.) to bow (of the legs).

SPUN OUT, SPUNNED OUT (adj.) exhausted.

SPURL, SPURDLE (vb.) to spread dung on the fields. Perhaps a sibillated form of 'purl'. See *Purdle*.

SQUAILER (n.) a throwing stick, loaded at one end with a lump of lead. *Squail* (vb.) to throw such a stick (but never used of throwing a stone).

SQUAT (vb.) to crush, to dent (adj.) crushed or dented. The word 'squat' in

R.S. is replaced in dialect by *Croupy* or by *Quat*.

SQUEAKER (n.) the smallest pig in a litter.

SQUINNY (vb.) to peep, to screw the eyes up when trying to make something out.

SQUISHY (adj.) soft, wet, swampy.

SQUITTLE (vb.) to whittle. A sibillated form.

SQUIVVER-HANDED (adj.) left-handed. Also found as *Squiffy-* or *Squippy-Handed*. See *Skiffy-Handed*.

SQWUG (n.) a squirrel. See *Scug*.

SRAMMED (adj.) very cold (of people). See *shrammed*.

STALE (n.) the handle of a broom, or of a garden tool such as a rake.

STARVED (adj.) perished with cold. *My old man he do starve I at nights wi' the cowld, 'cause he got a crooked leg, and he do sort o' cock un up 'snaw, and the draaft do get in under the bed-claus, and I be starved wi' the cowld.* Quoted in Goddard and Dartnell, A glossary of Wiltshire Words.

STEART (n.) the tang which fastens anything, the ring of a button, etc. I have always heard it used in terms of commiseration when, for instance, a splinter was removed and then described as 'a girt steart' or when a tooth came out, the roots of which were 'girt stearts'.

STICK (vb.) to stook, to pile sheaves in heaps to dry. Also found as *Stiching* or *Stocking*, but the usual word in the south-west is *Hiling*.

STICKY BUTTONS (n.) goosegrass, the small seed containers of which cling to the clothing.

STITCHING, STOCKING (vb.) See *Stick*.

STOGS (n. pl.) gaiters.

STONER (n.) a kind of a marble.

STOPING (vb.) removing ore from a lode in the Cornish tin mining industry.

STOWELL (n.) a root, the stump of a tree. A form of the word 'stool'. Still used in fruit growing in the sense 'root'.

STRADS (n. pl.) knee straps.

STREAM (vb.) to rinse. Cornwall.

STRICKLE (n.) a piece of wood used to level off the corn in a measure, or for other similar purposes. Also found as *Stritch*.

STROIL (n.) couch grass.

STUG (n.) a bin. Cornwall.

STUGGY (adj.) boggy.

SUANT (adj.) smooth, even, used both of motion and texture. A piece of cloth was said to be *Suant* if evenly woven, if not it was *Rowey*. Also found as *Shuant*.

SULLY (n.) a wooden plough. Also found as *Sole* or *Sull*.

SUMMERFACE (n.) freckles *Summerfolds*, *Summermoulds* (n. pl.) are also found.

SWEETHEART(S) (n.) goosegrass—because it clings.

TACK (n.) a shelf, as in *Chimney Tack* or *Clavy Tack*, a mantelpiece.

TACKLE (n.) material of any description, but especially food.

TAFFLED (adj.) tangled. Also *Tazzled*.

TAIL (n.) the whole skirt of a woman's dress.

TALLET (n.) a hay loft over a stable or similar building, or, sometimes, a specially built construction standing on staddle stones. This is word borrowed from Welsh, 'taflod', probably spread by itinerant workers.

TAZZLED (adj.) tangled. See *Taffled*.

TEART (adj.) tender, sore. A form of 'tart'.

TEFT (vb.) to test for weight. See *Heft*.

THILLER (n.) a shaft horse. See *Diller*.

THILLS (n. pl.) the shafts of a cart. See *Dills*.

THIRL, THIRDLE (adj.) hungry. Devonshire and Cornwall. Can also be used for 'lean and gaunt' of animals.

THRESHELS, usually a *Pair of Threshels* (n.) a flail. Also found as *Drashel(s)*.

THRIPPLES (n. pl.) the sides or ends of a waggon. See *Dripples*.

TIPPET (n.) a party game, more commonly known as 'Up Jenkins'.

TISTY-TOSTY (n.) a cowslip, or a cowslip ball. The ball was tossed by girls in the flat of the hand to ascertain the profession of their future husbands. See chapter 6.

TIZZICK (vb.) to wheeze. Perhaps a corruption of 'phthisis'.

TOLL (vb.) to entice, but usually used, in my experience, in the 'help to swallow', as in *Have some cheese to toll down the bread*.

TOMAHAWK (n.) a gardening tool either like a draw-hoe, but with a long, thin blade, similar to an adze, or with four tines set at right angles to the handle, and used in earthing up potatoes. Also known as a *Tommy Hacker*.

TOMMY (n.) food, especially when carried to the fields.

TOMTODDY (n.) a tadpole.

TOUSER (n.) a coarse apron, worn by women when working in the fields.

TRIG (vb.) to prop up, as, for example, a cart when the horse has been taken from the shafts, or 'This vase is broke, but it don't show when I do trig 'en up like this'.

TRINS, CALVES' TRINS (n. pl.) calves' stomach, used in cheese making.

TROUGH (n.) the kitchen sink, as well as the more usual forms used for feeding animals. A *sink* is an outside drain. *Trough* is invariably pronounced 'trow'. I hope that the participants of a recent car-rally were dialect-speaking, as the clue, 'an ecclesiastical drinking place' led to the village of Bishopstrow.

TRUCKLE (vb.) to roll, usually something small, like a marble.

TRUCKLES (n. pl.) sheep's or rabbit's dung.

TRULLEN (n.) a lane.

TUN (n.) the chimney of a house.

TUNDISH (n.) a funnel for pouring liquids into a container. Also found as *Tunigar* or *Tunnel*.

TUNDLE (vb.) used for smoke coming out of a chimney, 'the smoke is tundling out of the tun'. It is, possibly, a form of the verb *to tun*, meaning to pour liquid through a tundish into a vessel.

TURDSTOOL (n.) a patch of cow dung.

TURMET (n.) a turnip. A distortion of the original word. *Pasmet* is a similar distortion of 'parsnip'. *The Vly be on the Turmet* is a well-known west-country song.

TUTTY (n.) a flower, or a posy of flowers. *Tutty More* (n.) a flower root. In Hungerford, Berks, where old, picturesque customs have been maintained, the Tything Men carry poles wreathed in flowers, and are known as *Tutti-Men*, the poles being *Tutti-Poles*.

TUT WORK (n.) piece work in the Cornish tin mining industry.

TWIT (vb.) to tease. See *Betwit*.

UCK (vb.). Sometimes *Huck*. A form, it seems, of the verb 'to hook', but used in other senses in the south-west, e.g. of a cat scratching itself, of one cow prodding another with its horn, of removing weeds from between stones, or even, of spreading manure.

UCKLE (n.) a person, used contemptuously, 'silly uckle'.

UN- (prefix), used with words that do not have it in R.S., e.g. *Unthaw, Unempt(y)*.

URGE (vb.) to retch. A metathesised form.

VAMP (vb.) to walk about (usually in a critical sense, e.g. 'What good is she doing, vamping round the town like that').

VAR (vb.) to farrow.

VEER (n.) a furrow. VEER OUT (vb.) to mark out with a plough the lands to be ploughed.

VINNY (n.) mould. *Vinnied* (adj.) mouldy. Used for bread and cheese only.

VORSPUR (n.) the 'forespur', a hock of pork.

VORUS-NORUS (adj.) *A girt vorus-norus wench* a brazen girl. One of the corrupt forms of the Latin 'nolens-volens', willy-nilly.

VOSSEL (or more properly perhaps, *Foldsail*) (n.) a stake set in the ground to which a hurdle is attached. *Sail* (n.) the upright rod in a hurdle.

VRAKSEN (n. pl.) reeds. The word is 'wrack', as in 'bladderwrack' sea weed, with two plural endings, -s and -en. It illustrates the fact, in Somersetshire, until the last century, wr- at the beginning of a word was pronounced vr-.

VREATHE (vb.) to wreathe. Another example of the above.

WAKE, WALLOW WALLY (n.) a line of hay, raked ready to be put into cocks (**POOKED**).

WALLISH, WALLOWISH (adj.) in poor health, of poor quality.

WANT (n.) a mole pronounced 'oont in the northern part of our area. 'As fat as a want' is a common simile.

WATCHET, WETCHET (adj.) with wet feet. From 'wet-shod'.

WATTY-HANDED (adj.) left-handed.

WEATHE (adj.) pliable, of even consistency. Dough, when properly made is said to be *Weathe*.

WENCH (n.) one of the usual words for 'girl'. The jocular overtones of this word in Standard English are completely missing.

WENT (n.) a worn teasel. Cultivated teasels were extensively used in the cloth mills to raise the nap of pieces of cloth. Gloucestershire.

WEY the usual command in the southwest to stop a horse.

WHIPPENCE (n.) the swingle trees, the part of the plough to which the traces are attached.

WHISTLE (vb.) to neigh. Cornwall.

WHITE-LIVERED (adj.) pale and unhealthy looking.

WHITEMOUTH (n.) thrush, the infection of the mouth found in babies. It is also when one has received such a shock that one has a shivering sensation all over, even inside the mouth, *That gid you the whitemouth*.

WHIVER (vb.) to quiver, hover, flutter.

WHIZBIRD (n.) a term of reproach. Also found as *Husbird* and *Wozbird*.

The word is said to be derived from 'whore's brood' or 'whore's bird', but it has lost much of its sting and is used rather jocularly. I have been called a 'whizbird' many times, and I am sure that the people who used the term had no idea of the original meaning or they would never have used it. Goddard and Dartnell in the Glossary of Wiltshire Words append the following note: 'In his Dictionary of Provincial English, Wright defines this as 'a wasp', a mistake too amusing to be passed over'. Probably his informant heard a rustic who had got into a wasp's nest, and had been badly stung *danging they wosbirds*, and on asking what he meant by 'wosbirds' was told that they were the 'wopses' and not unnaturally concluded that the two words were synonyms'.

WICKER (vb.) to neigh, to burst out laughing. Also found as *Winker*.

WICKER (n.) the ear.

WILLIGOG (n.) a roundabout at a fair. This is a corruption of 'whirligig' and was applied to a rustic turnstile.

WILLOWIND (n.) Bindweed. See *Withywind*.

WIM (vb.) to winnow, to separate the loose husks and the grain after threshing.

WIMBLE (n.) an instrument, a little like a hand brace, used for twisting straw into rope.

WISK, WISP (n.) a sty on the eye. Found in a number of forms, such as *Wilk* or *Wilt*.

WITHY (n.) a willow tree.

WITHYWIND (n.) Bindweed, Convolvulus. This word comes in a number of forms, the first of which is *With* or *Withy*, reflecting the tough,

Wessex Dialect

pliable stem and root of the plant similar to the willow tree, or the osiers used in basket making; The second element is *Wind* or *Wine*, that is *Wind* has lost its -d after n, as so often happens in west-country words, and which indicates the way the stem winds around any support. See *Willowind*.

WORDLE (n.) the world. Not a metathesised form, but 'world' has lost its d (sound change 44), and then an excrescent d has been introduced.

YEWCUMS (n. pl.) hiccups.

YOP (vb.) to mouth at, to scold.

YORKS (n. pl.) straps tied just below the knee around the trousers to stop them trailing in the mud. See *Londonyorks*.

YUSEN (n.) a trough. Cornwall.

ZILT (n.) a salting trough.

ZOZZLED (adj.) drunk.

APPENDIX: LIST OF LINGUISTIC TERMS

ADJECTIVE: See PARTS OF SPEECH.

ADVERB: See PARTS OF SPEECH.

ANALOGY: A process by which one word is changed according to the pattern of another; e.g. the verb 'to snow' in English originally had the past tense 'snew', but was changed by analogy with the many weak verbs; in dialect 'to know' has undergone the same change.

ANGLO-SAXON: The language spoken in England between c. 500 A.D. and c. 1100 A.D. Also known as OLD ENGLISH.

ARTICLES: See PARTS OF SPEECH.

ASSIMILATION: A sound change by which one sound becomes more similar to a neighbouring sound; e.g. if we compare 'inedible' and 'impossible', we see that the [n] has become [m] under the influence of the labial ('lip') nature of p.

BLEND: The creation of a new word by combining parts of two others; e.g. 'annoyment'.

COGNATE: Derived from the same source; e.g. 'ant' and the dialect word 'emmet' are cognate as they both come from the Anglo-Saxon *æmete*.

CONTAMINATION: A change in one word under the influence of another; e.g. the metathesised form of 'retch', which should be 'urtch' becomes 'urge' under the influence of the verb of the same form in English; the word 'rafty', rancid (of bacon) becomes 'rufty' with a much wider meaning under the influence of 'rough'.

CONTINUOUS TENSE: A tense formed with the verb 'to be' and the present participle; e.g. I am working, you were saying.

CORNISH: The old language of Cornwall, a Celtic language, akin to Welsh and Breton, extinct as a spoken tongue since the eighteenth century.

COUNT NOUN: A COUNT NOUN is the name of an individual object, e.g. a book, a box, some pins; a MASS NOUN is the name of a material, e.g. some bread, aluminium. Some nouns can be both COUNT and MASS, e.g. a rubber, some rubber. MASS NOUNS have no plural.

DIALECT: A variant form of the language, which may be REGIONAL, OCCUPATIONAL (or TRADE) or CLASS. Although no real distinction exists, dialects are usually mutually intelligible, while languages are not.

DIPHTHONG: A vowel sound where the speech organs are not held still during the course of its production, thus changing the quality; the vowels in the words 'pane' and 'mine' are diphthongs. FALLING DIPHTHONG: A diphthong in which the first part bears the stress; all diphthongs in R.P. are falling.

RISING DIPHTHONG: A diphthong where the stress is on the second element; the dialect pronunciation of 'bean', i.e. 'byen' is a rising diphthong.

DIRECT OBJECT: See PARTS OF A SENTENCE.

DOUBLE PLURAL: A word which has two plural endings, because the original plural form was mistakenly construed as a singular, e.g. 'chick' (sing.) had, as its plural form 'chicken'. Now 'chicken' is sing. and we have a new (double) plural 'chickens'.

EXCRESCENT CONSONANT: An extra consonant added to a word either by mistake, e.g. 'cavaltry' (cavalry) or because it is easier to say, e.g. 'werdn' (were not).

FREQUENTATIVE TENSE: The present tense in English, such as 'I go' as opposed to 'I am going'.

FRONTING: Moving the raised part of the tongue, when producing a vowel sound, nearer the teeth.

GERMANIC LANGUAGES: A sub-group of the INDO-EUROPEAN family, which includes languages spoken in north and north-western Europe. English, German and the Scandinavian languages belong to this group.

GRAMMAR: That part of the study of language, which describes changes in the forms of words, e.g. 'see'/'saw', and the ways words may be combined into sentences.

GREAT VOWEL SHIFT: A series of changes in vowel sounds which took place in the fifteenth and subsequent centuries.

INFLEXION: A word ending which has grammatical meaning, e.g. the past tense ending -ed as in 'looked'.

INDO-EUROPEAN LANGUAGES: One of the major language families of the world, to which nearly all European languages, as well as many from the Middle East and India belong. All these have developed from one parent language.

INTERNATIONAL PHONETIC ALPHABET: A system of notation for recording sounds, and now widely accepted. (See chapter 2.)

INTONATION: The rise and fall of the voice as we speak.

INTRANSITIVE VERB: A verb used without a direct object (see PARTS OF THE SENTENCE), e.g. 'He is working hard'.

ISOGLOSS: A line drawn on a map showing the furthest point at which a linguistic feature has been recorded. BUNDLE OF ISOGLOSSES: Where several isoglosses coincide.

LABIAL CONSONANT: A consonant made with the lips, e.g. p, b, f.

MASS NOUN: See COUNT NOUN.

METANALYSIS: Mistaken division, by which, for example, 'a nadder' became 'an adder'.

METATHESIS: Shifting of consonants inside a word as when 'ask' is pronounced 'aks'.

MIDDLE ENGLISH: The English language between c. 1100 and c. 1500.

MINIMAL PAIRS: Two words differing in only one sound as 'pin' and 'bin'. These pairs can be used to prove the identity and number of sounds in a language.

MIXED PAST TENSE: A past tense formed by a vowel change and also by the addition of an ending, e.g. 'creep'/'crept'.

NOUN: See PARTS OF SPEECH.

Appendix:

PARTS OF SPEECH: Traditional grammar has eight parts of speech. Modern linguistic scientists have pointed out the weaknesses of this system, but have so far failed to supply a replacement. Here I shall give examples of the categories of traditional grammar.

ADJECTIVE: 'A describing word', *tall, intelligent, low*.

ADVERB: 'Modifies a verb' e.g. *warmly, neatly* or 'modifies an adjective', e.g. *very*.

ARTICLE: Traditionally, there are only two—*the* and *a/an*. In this head I have included all 'noun-introducers', e.g. *my, this*.

CONJUNCTION: 'A joining word', e.g. *and, but, because*.

NOUN: 'The name of a person, place or thing', e.g. *man, pen, Bristol*. This last, being the name of a particular place is a PROPER NOUN. See also COUNT NOUN, MASS NOUN.

PREPOSITION: Examples *with, in, because of*.

PRONOUN: 'A word which replaces a noun'. There are various kinds.

SUBJECT PRONOUN: *I, we, they*.

OBJECT PRONOUN: *me, us them*.

RELATIVE PRONOUN: *who, which, that*.

INTERROGATIVE PRONOUN: Who, what (when asking a question).

POSSESSIVE PRONOUN: *mine, yours*.

DEMONSTRATIVE PRONOUN: *This, that* (when used without a following noun, e.g. 'Look at this'.

VERB: 'A doing or being word', e.g. 'is' in 'He is ill', or 'spoke' in 'I spoke to my friend'.

PARTS OF A SENTENCE: Sentences may be divided into SUBJECT and PREDICATE. The SUBJECT tells us what or who is under consideration and the PREDICATE tells us what is said about it or him. In the predicate, we may find the VERB (as detailed above), the DIRECT OBJECT, the 'receiver' of the action of the verb, e.g. 'him' in 'I saw him', the INDIRECT OBJECT with verbs of 'saying, sending and giving', e.g. 'to him' in 'I spoke to him' or 'me' in 'He gave me a book'.

PHONEME: A distinctive sound in a language.

PHONOLOGY: The sound system of a language or dialect.

PREPOSITION: See PARTS OF SPEECH.

PRONOUN: See PARTS OF SPEECH.

RECEIVED PRONUNCIATION (R.P.), RECEIVED STANDARD (R.S.): The speech and language of 'educated' people, the kind of English used in books.

REGISTER: The facility we all have of adapting the tone of our discourse to the person we are addressing.

SIBILLATED WORD: One where S has been added to the beginning, e.g. 'plash' becomes 'splash'.

SPELLING PRONUNCIATION: A new pronunciation of a word which has been influenced by the spelling, e.g. the present day pronunciation of 'soldier' as compared with the older 'sojer'.

STRONG PAST TENSE: A past tense marked by a vowel change, e.g. 'sing'/'sung'.

Wessex Dialect

SUBJECT: See PARTS OF A SENTENCE.

SVARABHAKTI: 'Opening out', as when 'elm' is pronounced 'ellum'.

TENSE: Variant form of a verb, used to indicate the time at which the action taked place.

TRANSITIVE VERB: A verb which has a direct object.

VERB: See PARTS OF SPEECH.

VOCAL CORDS: A pair of muscular bands attached to the wall of the windpipe and which vibrate when in a certain position and the outgoing airstream passes over them, thus producing a musical tone called VOICE. When we use this tone we produce VOICED sounds, e.g. all vowels and [d], [v], [b]; when we do not, but rely on the hiss of passing air, we produce UNVOICED sounds e.g. [t], [f], [p].

VOWEL: A voiced sound which can be the centre of a syllable. To the usual list we must add [l] and [n] as in 'little' and 'rotten'.

WEAK PAST TENSE: A past tense formed by the addition of the ending -ed, e.g. 'walk'/'walked'.

WEST SAXON: A dialect of Anglo-Saxon, spoken in an area which corresponds roughly to the present-day counties of Devon, Somerset, Wilts, Hants, Berks, Dorset and Sussex.

For the general reader the following books provide a readable account of modern ideas of language and surveys of the history of our language and other languages.

S. POTTER, *Our Language* (Penguin) 1950.
             Language in the Modern World (Penguin) 1960.
C. L. BARBER, *The Story of Language* (Pan) 1964.

For those who wish to acquaint themselves with modern, analytical techniques in linguistics in more depth, there are a number of text-books available, e.g.
L. R. PALMER, *An Introduction to Modern Linguistics* (Macmillan) 1936.
H. A. GLEASON, *An Introduction to Descriptive Linguistics* (Holt) 1955.
S. POTTER, *Modern Linguistics* (Deutsch) 1957.
C. F. HOCKETT, *A Course in Modern Linguistics* (Macmillan) 1958.

An excellent description of modern English is given in the following:
BARBARA M. H. STRANG, *Modern English Structure* (Arnold) 1962.

For an account of the history of English, the reader should consult:
A. C. BAUGH, *A History of the English Language* (Appleton-Century-Crofts) 2nd. ed., 1957.

A concise and readable account of English place names is given in:
P. H. REANEY, *The Origin of English Place Names* (London) 1960.
The reader may also consult the various volumes dedicated to individual counties, published by the English Place Name Society.

The number of books dealing with English dialects as a whole is quite small.
W. SKEAT, *English Dialects from the Eighth Century to the Present Day* (Cambridge) 1911, though written by a pioneer of dialect studies, now has to be used with caution.
Two other accounts are more up-to-date:
G. L. BROOK, *English Dialects* (Deutsch) 2nd. ed. 1965:
M. WAKELIN, *English Dialects* (Athlone Press) 1977.
H. C. WYLDE, *A History of Modern Colloquial English* (Blackwell) 3rd. ed. 1936, while not concerned primarily with dialects, is a source of much useful information.

The Survey of English Dialects, carried out by the University of Leeds, initiated by Professor Eugen Dieth of the University of Zurich and Professor Harold Orton of the University of Leeds is indispensable in the detailed study of dialects today. So far the Introduction, containing the questionnaire used in the survey,

Wessex Dialect

and four volumes of replies have been published. Each of the volumes of replies consists of three separate books, that is 12 in all, a fact which shows the comprehensive nature of the survey. However, a good reading knowledge of the International Phonetic Alphabet is absolutely necessary to use these volumes, as the replies are recorded in it. Those that concern our area are

ORTON and DIETH, *Introduction* 1952.

ORTON and BARRY *The West Midland Counties* (contains Gloucestershire).

ORTON and WAKELIN *The Southern Counties* (contains Somersetshire, Wiltshire, Berkshire, Cornwall, Devonshire, Dorsetshire, and Hampshire).

All are published by E. J. Arnold.

Of the works published in the nineteenth century we may start with A. J. ELLIS, *On Early English Pronunciation*, Part V: 'The Existing Phonology of English Dialects' (Early English Text Society) 1889, later published by the English Dialect Society.

The works published by the English Dialect Society, and which concern our area are as follows:

F. T. ELWORTHY, *The Dialect of West Somerset*. 1875.

PRINCE L. L. BONAPARTE, *On the Dialects of eleven Southern and South-Western Counties*. 1877.

F. T. ELWORTHY, *An Outline of the Grammar of the Dialect of West Somerset*. 1877.

W. SKEAT (ed.) Five Reprinted Glossaries (including Wiltshire). 1879.

F. T. ELWORTHY (ed.) *Exmoor Scolding and Courtship in Specimens of English Dialects*. 1879.

M. A. COURTNEY *A Glossary of Words in Use in Cornwall*, 1: West Cornwall. 1880.

VARIOUS AUTHORS, *Five Original Glossaries* (including one from the Isle of Wight).

REV. H. FRIEND, *Devonshire Plant Names*. 1882.

SIR W. H. COPE (Bart.), *Hampshire Words and Phrases*. 1883.

F. T. ELWORTHY *A Glossary of West Somerset Words*. 1886.

MAJOR LOWSLEY, *Berkshire Words*.

J. D. ROBERTSON, *Dialect Words used in the County of Gloucester* (ed. Lord Moreton). 1890.

R. PEARSE CHOPE, *The Dialect of Hartland, Devonshire*. 1891.

G. E. DARTNELL and REV. E. H. GODDARD, *A Glossary of Wiltshire Words*. 1893. (This book contains a reprint of a short manuscript, then in the hands of a Mr. W. Cunnington, and referred to by the authors as the 'Cunnington Manuscript. The authors believe it to have been compiled 'about the middle of last century'.)

These books are mainly glossaries, but they contain a few observations on grammar and pronunciation, often in a rather disjointed way. They were published for the Society by Henry Frowde.

More technical in their approach are several monographs concerning the dialect of a certain area. Once again, it is necessary to have a good knowledge of the International Phonetic Alphabet, or to be willing to familiarise oneself with the particular kind of phonetic notation that the author uses.

E. KRUISINGA, *A Grammar of the Dialect of West Somerset*, Bonn 1905.

J. KJEDERQVIST, *The Dialect of Pewsey* (*Wiltshire*) Transactions of the Philological Society 1903–1906.

B. WIDÉN, *Studies in the Dorset Dialect* (Lund) 1949.

Among older works may be cited:

F. GROSE, *A Provincial Glossary; with a Collection of Local Proverbs and Popular Superstitions* (London) New ed. 1811.

J. O. HALLIWELL, *A Dictionary of Archaic and Provincial Words* (London) 1848. This book contains examples of the dialect of every county.

In addition, many counties publish bibliographies in which are listed other dialect articles and writings. These can usually be obtained from the local library, or from the library of the local archaeological society.